The Data Platform Handbook

Architecture, Design, and Best Practices

Jane Estrada

Technics Publications

SEDONA, ARIZONA

115 Linda Vista, Sedona, AZ 86336 USA

https://www.TechnicsPub.com

Edited by Sadie Hoberman
Cover design by Lorena Molinari

First Printing 2025

Copyright © 2025 by Jane Estrada

ISBN, print ed.	9781634626736
ISBN, Kindle ed.	9781634626743
ISBN, PDF ed.	9781634626804

Library of Congress Control Number: 2025931546

Contents

Figures

Tables

Introduction

In this book, we will explore the technology-agnostic design of a Data Platform and the key components required to ensure its success. Through this journey, Data Stewards, Data Custodians, Data Architects, Solution Architects, Data Engineers, and Data Governance professionals will gain valuable insights into how a well-designed Data Platform can address modern data challenges and unlock the full potential of enterprise data.

Data is valuable only when it is meaningful and accessible. A Data Platform serves as a centralized, integrated ecosystem that enables mid-to-large enterprises to distribute, manage, and leverage data for intelligent, data-driven decision-making. A well-designed Data Platform is fundamental to executing an enterprise's data strategy, providing a unified foundation where technology, processes, and governance frameworks come together to drive business agility and innovation.

Overview of the Chapters

- **Chapters 1 & 2** introduce the concept of the Data Platform and its benefits to an enterprise. The evolution from databases to data warehouses, data lakes, and data meshes is explored, providing historical context for today's data architectures. These chapters also outline the numerous benefits of a well-structured Data Platform, equipping Data Management leaders with key insights to make a compelling business case.

- **Chapter 3** delves into the practical methodologies that contribute to a successful Data Platform. A strong vision is essential for turning ideas into reality, and this chapter highlights the foundational building blocks—including MDM, data strategy, data models, federated responsibility, and architecture—that must be considered when designing or enhancing a Data Platform.

- **Chapter 4** focuses on data models within a Data Platform. Data modeling has become a contentious topic due to its complexity and time commitment. This chapter explores the evolution of data models, their role in modern Data Platforms, and the adoption of a Common Data Model as a viable alternative to traditional, lengthy modeling practices.

- **Chapters 5 & 6** examine the structured layers of a Data Platform, including raw, standardized, and consumer-specific layers, as well as producer and consumer onboarding. These layers create flexibility to accommodate diverse use cases. Additionally, the role of an onboarding team in facilitating producer and consumer onboarding is discussed, emphasizing a federated, metadata-driven approach to Data Platform management.

By applying the principles and methodologies outlined in this book, enterprises can design, implement, and manage a future-ready Data Platform that transforms data into a strategic asset. Furthermore, these concepts can guide vendor selection, help organizations evaluate third-party Data Platform solutions, or serve as a blueprint for building a custom Data Platform using in-house expertise.

## CHAPTER ONE

What is a Data Platform?

What is a data platform? It is a central integrated ecosystem designed to distribute data required by strategic business initiatives. A data platform is used to standardize fragmented data across multiple data sources, provide the capability to track a data element's behavior across all channels, and enable intelligent data-driven decisions based on facts. A good data platform is no longer a nice to have; it is a necessity to enable data governance. By centralizing the data required for business initiatives, organizations eliminate point-to-point integrations that unnecessarily run up IT costs and cause misinformation.

The concept of a data platform reflects the ever-evolving need for enterprises to collect, store, and utilize data effectively. This evolution began in the early 1960s when Charles Bachman introduced the Integrated Data Store (IDS), a pioneering system in database management. IDS stored files on disk and allowed developers to access and manipulate data through a Data Manipulation Language (DML), laying the foundation for structured data handling. By the late 1960s, IBM advanced these ideas by introducing the Integrated Management System (IMS), which remains a standard database system today. IMS was designed around a hierarchical database model, offering a more structured and efficient approach to organizing and retrieving data. In 1970, Edgar Codd revolutionized database management by developing the relational database model, an advancement on IMS. This model introduced tables and relationships to organize data, emphasizing flexibility and scalability. Codd's relational model became the cornerstone of modern database systems, enabling a structured and systematic approach to data storage and retrieval that continues to influence database technologies. The relational view of data describing the structure and relationships improved the organization of the data because it was superior to machine representation. "A further advantage of the relational view is that it forms a sound basis for treating derivability, redundancy, and consistency of relations."[1]

Inmon and Kimball Data Warehouse Design

As the need to access organization data increased, the idea of a data warehouse with relational data models became popular in the 1980s. Bill Inmon, considered to be the father of data warehousing, coined the term "data warehouse" and "developed the concept of Corporate Information Factory (CIF), an enterprise view of an organization's data of which Data Warehousing plays one part … Inmon's approach to data warehouse design focuses on a centralized data repository modeled to the Third Normal Form. Inmon feels using strong relational modeling leads to enterprise-wide consistency, facilitating easier development of individual data marts to better serve the needs of the departments using the actual data. This approach differs in some respects to the 'other' father of Data Warehousing, Ralph Kimball."[2] Inmon's CIF architecture appears in Figure 2.

While Inmon's approach to Data Warehousing is "top-down," focusing on centralized relational data models in a Third Normal Form (3NF) structure, Kimball championed a contrasting "bottom-up" approach. Kimball's method de-centralizes data into data marts built using star schemas that are designed to support specific business processes. Figure 1

---

[1] Codd, E. F. "A Relational Model of Data for Large Shared Data Banks." *University of Pennsylvania Engineering*, June 1970, www.seas.upenn.edu/~zives/03f/cis550/codd.pdf.

[2] Kempe, Shannon. "A Short History of Data Warehousing." *Dataversity*, 29 Jan. 2024, www.dataversity.net/a-short-history-of-data-warehousing/.

shows Kimball's dimensional data warehouse, where centrally normalizing data using a 3NF data model is not required. The presentation layer or data marts, tailored to individual business processes, are created using dimensional modeling (e.g., star schemas). These marts are integrated to form a broader data warehouse. This approach prioritizes faster deployment and flexibility, making it ideal for business process-specific reporting. Kimball's conformed dimensions can be used to create "common, standardized, master dimensions that are managed once in the Extract, Transformation, and Load (ETL) system and then reused by multiple fact tables. Conformed dimensions deliver consistent descriptive attributes across dimensional models. They support the ability to drill across and integrate data from multiple business processes."[3]

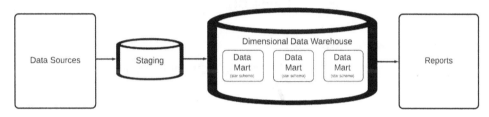

Figure 1: Kimball's dimensional data warehouse[4]

Figure 2: Inmon's Corporate Information Factory (CIF)

---

[3] "Enterprise Data Warehouse Bus Architecture." *Kimball Group*, Kimball Group, www.kimballgroup.com/data-warehouse-business-intelligence-resources/kimball-techniques/kimball-data-warehouse-bus-architecture/. Accessed 8 Dec. 2024.

[4] Ross, Margy. "Differences of Opinion." *Kimball Group*, 26 Jan. 2016, www.kimballgroup.com/2004/03/differences-of-opinion/.

Advantages of the Inmon Method

- **Normalized Unified View of Enterprise Data:** Inmon's approach provides a comprehensive, centralized, and normalized view of the enterprise data. When combined with a mature **Master Data Management (MDM)** system for products and customers, this architecture effectively supports sophisticated, cross-departmental projects.

- **Scalability and Simplicity:** The architecture is scalable to accommodate evolving business and system requirements. One of its key strengths lies in the simplicity of updating the data warehouse, as each data element is stored in only one place, minimizing redundancy and complexity.

- **Improved data quality:** Using a **3NF** data model reduces data loading complexity and improves data quality by eliminating redundancies and ensuring data consistency.

Advantages of the Kimball Method

- **Fast Delivery of Business Intelligence (BI) Projects**: Kimball's dimensional data warehouse, using star schemas, enables faster delivery of BI projects by reducing the number of layers through which data must travel.

- **Star schema**: The denormalized star schema structure enhances performance for report generation.

- **Ease of Maintenance**: Maintaining a Kimball-style data warehouse requires only a small team, making it a cost-effective solution for organizations with limited resources.

- **Conformed Dimensions**: Conformed dimensions allow data to be aggregated or drilled down across multiple star schemas, enabling the reusability of dimensional data across reporting capabilities.

Both approaches are still relevant today; enterprises can often blend these methodologies to balance quick insights and long-term strategic data management. As Inmon describes it, "When you use the Kimball approach you get data fast and fit for analytics. When you use the Inmon approach you end up with corporate data."[5]

Data Lake Architecture

As we moved into the 21st century, the use cases for structured and unstructured data within organizations expanded dramatically. Traditional data warehouses were increasingly seen as too slow to develop, costly to maintain, and incapable of handling unstructured data or delivering the performance required for advanced analytics. The data lake architecture emerged as a solution in response to these limitations. Data lakes provide low-cost, high-speed data storage capable of centralizing vast amounts of both structured and unstructured data in their native or file-based formats. This flexibility enables analytics, reporting, and data science use cases to be more effective than traditional data warehouses. However, many data lakes failed to meet their potential and became data swamps due to several challenges:

- Lacking metadata and standardized data structures makes it difficult to organize and understand the data.

---

[5] Inmon, Bill. "Kimball vs Inmon Redux." *LinkedIn*, 21 June 2024, www.linkedin.com/pulse/kimball-vs-inmon-redux-bill-inmon-gatic/.

- Ensuring data security and governance in such an open environment proves complex.

- Querying data stored in a variety of formats often results in poor performance and difficulty extracting actionable insights.

These shortcomings highlighted the need for new architectures and methodologies, leading to the evolution of modern solutions like the lakehouse and data mesh, which aim to combine the strengths of data warehouses and data lakes while addressing their weaknesses.

It became evident that enterprise data serves purposes far beyond traditional reporting and analytics. Data created and utilized in business transactions is now essential for regulatory compliance, operational processes, and real-time decision-making. Moreover, data has been recognized as a strategic asset, offering the potential for significant competitive advantage. Advances in big data technologies, Artificial Intelligence (AI), and cloud storage have further accelerated this evolution, enabling enterprises to process, analyze, and store massive volumes of structured and unstructured data more efficiently. Simultaneously, the emergence of the Data Office introduced a more centralized and strategic approach to data governance, management, and utilization, further solidifying the role of data as a critical business enabler.

Lakehouse Architecture

The lakehouse architecture corrects the shortcomings of the data lake. The lakehouse architecture has the data warehouse on top of the data lake with metadata to better understand the meaning of the data. Figure 3 shows the evolution of lakehouse architecture, which improves data quality, faster delivery, and better performance. Vendors such as Databricks, Snowflake, and Amazon Redshift offer out-of-the-box lakehouse solutions, making them popular in many enterprises today.

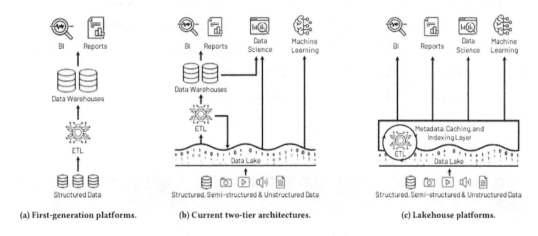

(a) First-generation platforms. (b) Current two-tier architectures. (c) Lakehouse platforms.

Figure 3: Evolution from first generation data warehouses to lakehouse platforms[6]

Medallion Architecture

The medallion architecture describes a series of data layers that denote the quality of data stored in the lakehouse.[7] While the concept behind the medallion architecture is rooted in traditional data architecture principles, particularly Inmon's CIF, which emphasizes progressive refinement and data quality improvement, the term "medallion architecture" was coined and popularized by Databricks. It reflects a modern adaptation of traditional ideas to fit the scalability and flexibility of the lakehouse paradigm. The medallion

---

[6] Armbrust, Michael, et al. "Lakehouse: A New Generation of Open Platforms That Unify Data Warehousing and Advanced Analytics." *11th Annual Conference on Innovative Data Systems Research (CIDR '21)*, Jan. 2021, www.cidrdb.org/cidr2021/papers/cidr2021_paper17.pdf.

[7] "What Is the Medallion Lakehouse Architecture?" *Azure Databricks | Microsoft Learn*, 1 Mar. 2024, www.learn.microsoft.com/en-us/azure/databricks/lakehouse/medallion.

architecture takes "a multi-layered approach to building a single source of truth for enterprise data products. This architecture guarantees atomicity, consistency, isolation, and durability as data passes through multiple layers of validations and transformations before being stored in a layout optimized for efficient analytics. The terms bronze (raw), silver (validated), and gold (enriched) describe the quality of the data in each of these layers. It is important to note that the medallion architecture does not replace other dimensional modeling techniques. Schemas and tables within each layer can take on a variety of forms and degrees of normalization depending on the frequency and nature of data updates and the downstream use cases for the data."[8]

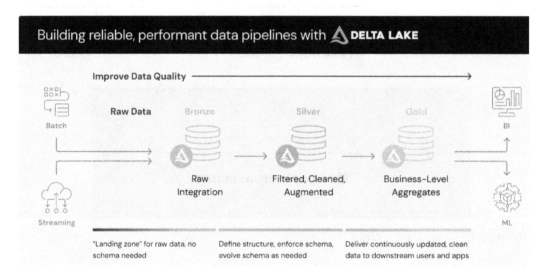

Figure 4: Databricks Delta Lake technology using the medallion architecture to organize data in lakehouse

---

[8] "What Is a Medallion Architecture?" *Databricks*, www.databricks.com/glossary/medallion-architecture.

Data Mesh Methodology

Data mesh is a decentralized approach that promotes data as a product by distributing responsibilities to business owners so that subject matter experts own the data. Data mesh is an inter-connected set of data domains owned and managed by business owners who have domain-specific expertise. This approach reduces silos and promotes federated collaborative data management. Unlike monolithic IT architectures, data mesh focuses on data domain-driven products that capture real-time data from systems of record and facilitate seamless data pipelines to support diverse enterprise needs. It enables scalable, flexible, and agile data distribution that aligns with the needs of modern businesses. Data mesh principles can be effectively implemented within various architectures, such as lakehouse, by distributing the ownership of data products to domain-specific teams. While many of data mesh's principles have been part of enterprise data strategies for years, Zhamak Dehghani of Thoughtworks formally introduced the methodology and coined the term "data mesh" in 2019. Her work has popularized this approach, providing a structured framework for its adoption.[9]

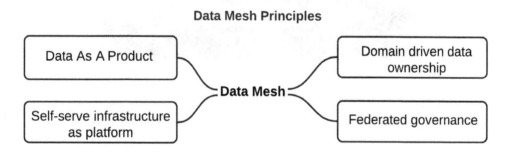

Figure 5: Data mesh principles allow for federated collaboration[10]

---

[9] "What Is a Data Mesh?" *Oracle Cloud Infrastructure*, www.oracle.com/ca-en/integration/what-is-data-mesh/.

[10] Woodie, Alex. "Data Meshes Set to Spread in 2022." *Datanami*, 21 Jan. 2022, www.datanami.com/2022/01/21/data-meshes-set-to-spread-in-2022/.

Data Fabric Architecture

Data Fabric architecture uses virtualization, knowledge graph, metadata, AI, and Machine Learning (ML) to integrate data from various systems of record together to provide a unified view of the data while minimizing copies of the data. "In layman's terms, a data fabric says that you don't need to centralize data, but put things in order where this data resides. So, instead of replacing or rebuilding the existing infrastructure, you add a new, ML-powered abstraction layer on top of the underlying data sources, enabling various users to access and manage the information they need without duplication."[11]

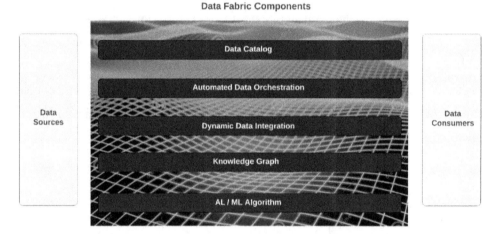

Figure 6: Components of the data fabric architecture

---

[11] "What Is Data Fabric: Architecture, Principles, Advantages, and Ways to Implement." *AltexSoft*, 22 Aug. 2022, www.altexsoft.com/blog/data-fabric/.

Data Platform

There is no universally agreed-upon definition of a data platform, and searching online yields varying interpretations without consistency. This book presents a definition and architecture based on first hand experience designing and working with data platforms in the financial and telecommunication industries. A data platform integrates and builds upon the traditional frameworks of data warehouses, data lakes, and data meshes to create a unified, centralized solution for enterprise data needs. Without such a platform, enterprises often resort to disconnected, siloed tools and data stores, which result in inefficiencies such as duplicate data, poor governance, and increased complexity. Figure 7 illustrates the core foundational elements of a data platform. When implemented with robust processes and methodologies, these elements transform enterprise data into a strategic asset. Once the foundation is established, the platform can evolve by adding advanced features, as shown in Figure 8, enabling enterprises to extract insights and power business initiatives more effectively.

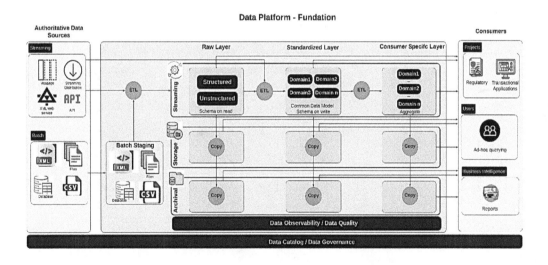

Figure 7: Data platform showing the fundamental features

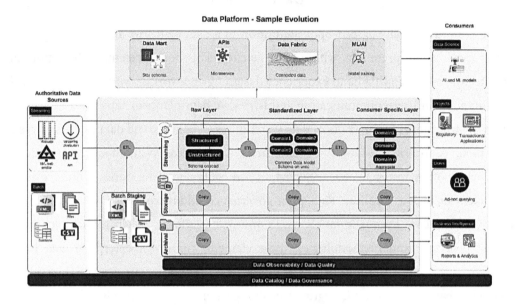

Figure 8: Data platform showing the fundamental features plus some possible additions

## CHAPTER TWO

Benefits of a Data Platform

As with any non-customer-facing initiative, pitching and demonstrating the benefits of a data platform to business units can be challenging. A data platform does not directly impact customer satisfaction or revenue stream and requires significant initial investment to get started. It is a backend enabler, a foundational solution, that sets up the enterprise to achieve many benefits, but for those who are not data experts, it is hard to appreciate the short- and long-term vision. As architects and product owners of a data platform, it is essential to grasp the vision and benefits of the platform to communicate its value effectively to stakeholders and ensure alignment across the organization. Let's explore some of the benefits.

One-Stop-Shop for Data

Consolidating governed, standardized business data domains into a single data platform makes it easier to access data when needed. Data centralization allows for a quick response to changing business needs by providing flexible and scalable data processing and storage capabilities. For project teams, it takes less time to do data source analysis, allowing the data analyst to quickly validate the data in the platform to ensure it is appropriate for their project use cases and significantly speed up delivery. Following the domain-driven approach means the data owners manage their data products for their domains, and project data analysts and architects can leverage their expertise to the fullest to develop well-informed solutions.

The data platform is a vital tool for the enterprise to accomplish its data strategy. When the data strategy is applied in a well-designed data platform, it enables the agile realization of the enterprise goals in a single place using a consolidated set of technologies and processes. The typical data strategy objectives, such as data security, integrity, regulatory compliance, governance, controls, analytics, modeling, etc., are much easier to implement in a data platform than in many applications spread across the enterprise. Figure 9 shows an enterprise integration landscape with and without a data platform. Centralizing data arranged by data domains eliminates data duplication and point-to-point integration, setting the path to numerous benefits.

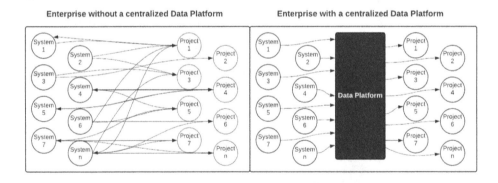

Figure 9: Data platform streamlines the integration, eliminating silos and point-to-point integrations

Better Decision Making

When all the essential data is centralized and managed, intelligent reporting can be created more quickly using visuals displayed in dashboards. Additionally, mining data leads to potential business opportunities. In enterprises without a centralized data platform, obtaining reliable metrics is difficult because multiple data sources managed by different teams must be combined to meet a specific use case. When data begins to be duplicated multiple times, it is difficult to govern, and a consistent unified view becomes impossible.

Federated Collaboration

A federated or decentralized approach to a data platform fosters collaboration across technical, data management, and business teams. This method promotes a collaborative approach for collecting, standardizing, and distributing data, requiring cross-departmental participation for the collective benefit. Technical teams contribute development expertise, data management teams enforce data policies, and business teams define data in business-relevant terms. This powerful three-way collaboration organized by data domains produces data that serves the enterprise effectively. The expertise and ownership aligned by domains enable project teams to tap into business insights that may otherwise be difficult to access. This approach aligns with the principles of the data mesh architecture discussed earlier.

Reusable Data

A data platform's common data model in the standardized layer follows data mesh best practices by organizing the data storage by data domain in a normalized format. This means the data is stored in the most granular format, facilitating many downstream projects to consume the data and aggregate it to be fit for purpose. As the data platform becomes the single source of truth, enterprises benefit from cost savings and efficient project deliveries.

Common View

Following the principles of Inmon's CIF, the data platform takes the data from source systems and transforms it into a common format (common data model) for easy consumption in the standardized layer. Moreover, the common data model enforces a common language, providing a common view of data from disparate sources. For example, systems 1, 2, and 3 can use different labels to refer to a customer. This can be confusing and requires time-consuming analysis before projects can ingest this data for their usage. To eliminate this issue, the common data model in the data platform defines a single governed data element for a client with a good business definition so all three systems can consistently populate the standardized data element. Now, projects wanting this data have a homogeneous common view of a customer.

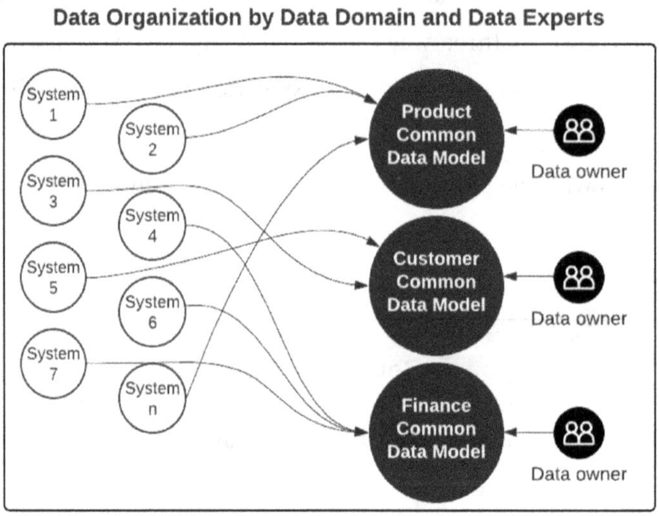

Figure 10: A common data model in the standardized layer created a single enterprise view of the data domain

Improved Data Quality

It is much easier to implement data quality checks in a central data platform than it is to implement in disparate source systems that have varying technology stacks and source-specific labels that are hard to understand. As the data quality is monitored and improved in the data platform, enterprises can make strategic decisions and avoid embarrassing, costly data errors.

Metadata Driven Project Delivery

Business and technical metadata collection is a critical part of the data platform. Metadata answers fundamental questions such as

- What data is available?
- Which systems have the data required?
- How does the data flow through the enterprise?
- How do I access the data?
- What transformations are applied to the data between the source and common data model?

Metadata to explain the data in the data platform is foundational and the most important pillar to build trust in the data and to enable federated collaboration. Easily accessible metadata promotes self-serve and trust in data.

Benefit to Data Producers

Source system teams frequently face challenges when multiple downstream teams request customized data feeds for specific projects, creating numerous point-to-point pipelines that become increasingly complex to maintain. A data platform addresses this issue by centralizing data access, allowing downstream teams to retrieve data from a single, centralized source. This approach lets producers focus on core tasks rather than managing bespoke data feeds. In this model, producers build one pipeline to the data platform, allowing any project requiring data to access it directly, as shown in Figure 9.

Benefits to Consumer Projects

In our data-driven world, most projects initiated at any enterprise need data to achieve their goals. For instance, regulatory and reporting projects need good quality data from all the relevant sources to automate their data feeds. Data platforms with a common data format speed up the integration and analysis timelines so regulatory projects can keep up with the ever-changing requirements without reputational loss or incurring hefty fines.

There are many other benefits to creating a data platform in the corporate world. Often, the Chief Data Office focuses its efforts on building an efficient data platform so it can get on with governing the data for the enterprise. There is so much to gain from building a data platform to centralize the data.

## CHAPTER THREE

Methodology for the Data Platform

Thanks to the explosion of data in recent years, most large-sized enterprises acknowledge the need for shared, controlled data and have established data platforms, data lakes, or data warehouses. However, there are still many lessons to learn in standing up shared data that is scalable and reuseable by multiple business areas. For example, at one of the Capital Markets financial institutions, the Risk department sponsored a Warehouse, which led to aggregated data with calculations satisfying Risk use cases but not Finance, Operations, HR, or Trading. This risk-specific data warehouse created a siloed view that couldn't be used by all regulatory use cases, and so a new program had to be initiated to create a data platform with granular data that could be aggregated as required by the different business areas. A practical methodology that outlines the vision, architecture, standards, and detailed approach before developing is an important step in setting up a data platform that will stand the test of time.

Master Data Management (MDM)

A robust Master Data Management (MDM) implementation is pivotal to the success of a data platform, arguably more so than any other foundational pillar. MDM, such as product and customer, are critical parts of any data management practice. Master data creates a consistent, unified view of core entities like customers, products, locations, and employees, all essential for streamlined operations, analytics, and effective decision-making. Without a strong MDM foundation, maintaining high-quality data within the data platform is challenging, if not impossible.

As data from diverse sources accumulates in the data platform, its value and meaningfulness depend on the presence of global MDM identifiers, such as customer IDs. These identifiers enrich and standardize records, significantly enhancing data quality. An MDM ID serves as an enterprise-wide unique identifier for a specific master data record, enabling organizations to consistently track and manage these entities across various systems. This ensures all systems reference a single, verified source of truth. For example, a customer may possess multiple IDs across different systems, but the MDM ID consolidates these into a single, comprehensive "master" profile for that customer.

Ideally, MDM solutions should be established as a prerequisite for a data platform. MDM applications excel at cleansing, matching, de-duplication, and operational maintenance of master data, leveraging specialized tools and rules designed for these tasks. Performing these functions within the data platform is possible but suboptimal due to the complexity and specificity of MDM requirements. In a well-designed ecosystem, the MDM application should publish cleansed, high-quality master data to the data platform, which serves as the central hub for data distribution. The data platform, in turn, ensures that this master data is accessible for strategic business initiatives, supporting analytics, reporting, and other enterprise-wide objectives. By delineating these roles, MDM for data cleansing and unification and the data platform for data distribution, organizations can maximize the efficiency and effectiveness of their data management practices.

Data Strategy

DAMA-DMBOK®, published by DAMA International, states, "A strategy is a set of choices and decisions that together chart a high-level course of action to achieve high-level goals."[12] A data strategy is unique to each enterprise but typically defines core pillars, as depicted in Figure 11 from DAMA. It is a comprehensive plan for managing an organization's data, including technology, processes, and policies that guide data acquisition, storage, distribution, and usage. Since the data platform is integral to the data strategy, it is advantageous to establish an enterprise-level data strategy first, as it provides the necessary context for the data platform's role. The data strategy illustrates how elements like the data platform, Master Data Management (MDM), and data quality collectively support the broader business strategy.

Figure 11: DMBOK (Data Management Body of Knowledge) wheel as defined by DAMA International

---

12 "DMBOK - Data Management Body of Knowledge." *DAMA*, 3 Apr. 2024, www.dama.org/cpages/body-of-knowledge.

When there is a lack of data strategy, one or more of the following can happen:

- It may become difficult to get the business buy in for a data platform, since the business cannot understand the overall enterprise plan for the data.

- In the absence of a data strategy, organizations may prioritize the development of the data platform without first implementing an MDM strategy. This leads to suboptimal outcomes, such as inconsistencies in master data, poor data quality, and challenges in achieving a unified view of core business entities.

- Enterprises may end up with multiple data lakes, data warehouses, and data platforms, each serving isolated business needs rather than being integrated at the business area or enterprise level.

- Ad hoc development often occurs when teams create siloed solutions to immediate business requirements. This fragmented approach can result in data duplication, inconsistencies, and heightened security risks, as data governance is typically deprioritized in such scenarios.

- Collaboration from business partners to contribute their expertise may become challenging when there is a lack of plan aligning the business and technology teams along business drivers.

While a well-defined data strategy provides the ideal foundation for building a data platform, there are instances where teams may need to proceed without one. A grassroots approach can still be effective in such scenarios, provided the platform's architecture is designed to accommodate future evolution. Success also hinges on the commitment of all stakeholders to continuously refine and mature the platform over time.

Vision

The overall vision for the data platform as well as the guiding principles, should be clearly expressed and published in an easily accessible location. When there is an enterprise-level data strategy, the vision and principles should align with the overall data strategy for alignment and consistency. The vision statement should briefly introduce the main purpose of the data platform. Here is one example of a wealth management data platform:

> *Wealth data platform enables the wealth data strategy to provide a unified standard data flow for wealth management initiatives.*

Guiding Principles

Guiding principles for the data platform are high-level guidelines that direct how the teams operate and make decisions. They provide a framework for action and behavior in alignment with the enterprise's mission, vision, and values outlined in the data strategy. Since each enterprise is unique, carefully consider the guiding principles that match the business strategy. Here are some examples:

- The data platform enables self-service for producers and consumers.

- The data platform should support agile data management.

- The architecture patterns support phased development so the data platform can be continuously scaled for performance and extended with additional features.

- Data coverage for a data domain must be holistic.

- Data domain driven architecture means data ingestion into the data platform needs to be organized by data domain. When onboarding a data domain, incomplete data is not kept in the platform; this means all critical data elements for the data domain must be onboarded.

- A common governed set of vocabulary is used in all aspects of the data platform.

- All the nomenclature, such as data attributes, must be governed by business experts and approved by Data owners or the Data office.

- Data is a shared asset, and all business units use the data in the data platform.

- Granular data must be ingested into the data platform for each data domain so aggregations are possible when required.

Federated versus Centralized Responsibility

Should the data platform have centralized, federated, or hybrid responsibility? Deciding on a solution approach is best since it heavily impacts team structures. However, becoming fixated on this issue without agreement on an approach is unnecessary because it can evolve from centralized to hybrid to federated responsibility over time. A federated approach is ideal since it fosters collaboration between business, technical, and data teams. However, culture can kill progress, and some corporate cultures are not ready for a completely federated approach. Thus, adopting the appropriate method suitable for the culture is best.

Figure 12 illustrates a sample centralized team composition. The centralized team identifies authoritative data sources based on consumer requirements and collaborates with them to onboard the data into the platform. As a result of centralizing infrastructure, governance, data pipeline development, support, and domain expertise, the team can grow significantly over time. Building a team with expertise across all domains is crucial in establishing access to subject-matter experts within the business areas to validate data analysis, the common data model, and data quality. While centralizing domain expertise and engaging business owners—who may not be directly responsible for the data platform—can be challenging, it is achievable. This approach is often favored in the early stages of the data platform, especially when the benefits are not yet evident to business leaders, who may be reluctant to support a federated approach.

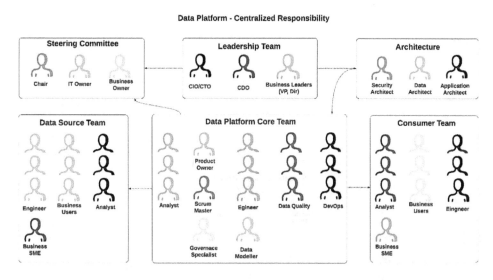

Figure 12: Sample composition and interaction of a centralized data platform team. The core team can easily grow large enough to support all the data domains in the enterprise.

In the federated approach, the responsibility for the data is decentralized to leverage domain expertise. Business domain experts and owners become integral to the data platform, leading to better quality data. Infrastructure maintenance and support are centralized, but data ownership, development of data pipelines, and governance lie with teams with domain expertise. Enabling a self-serve data platform requires constant education; it takes time for source and consumer teams to understand the data platform process, technologies, and tools. The journey to becoming federated can take time, but it has many business benefits:

1. Data is democratized with shared responsibility.
2. Businesses can directly influence the evolution of data practices to support their strategy.
3. Since the data platform team is small, there is cost efficiency.
4. Collaboration between technology and business teams leads to better solutions.
5. Business users get improved access to data to make decisions.
6. A Federated data domain-driven approach works well with a Microservices architecture.

Figure 13 shows a sample composition and interaction of a federated data platform team.

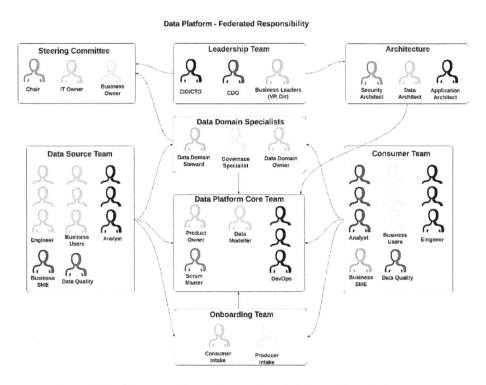

Figure 13: Sample composition and interaction of a federated data platform team

The data platform team is small because most of the work is done by source and consumer teams with domain expertise. Data domain specialists assist these teams in ensuring the correct process and governance are followed. In 2018, Zhamak Dehghani, Director of Technology at Thoughtworks, popularized decentralized governance by introducing the data mesh concept,[13] laying out the principles and advantages of decentralized governance. Table 1 below summarizes the differences and similarities between federated and centralized responsibility.

Team	Centralized Responsibility	Federated Responsibility
Steering Committee	A C-level sponsor chairs the Data Governance Steering Committee, which includes key business and IT leaders from various departments, as well as the Data Governance leaders. The Committee is responsible for reviewing, approving, and resolving data governance policies, as well as overseeing normative resources to ensure consistent data management across the enterprise. The executive sponsor is the ultimate decision maker.	The Data Governance Steering Committee is chaired by key C-level business leaders from various departments in collaboration with IT leaders, business leaders, and data domain specialists. The committee is tasked with reviewing, approving, and resolving data governance policies, as well as overseeing normative resources to ensure consistent data management across the enterprise. C-level business leaders share decision making.
Leadership Team	IT and business leadership team members provide strategic input on the overall development and performance of the data governance framework. But the executive sponsor is the ultimate decision maker.	IT and business leadership team members provide strategic direction and oversight on their data domain and contribute to the overall development and performance of the data governance framework.
Architecture	A Centralized Architecture team ensures the strategic direction aligns with the enterprise roadmap and creates blueprints that construction teams use to build a given structure. Architects have the final say on the IT direction.	Architects assigned to data domains aligned to their respective IT and business leaders ensure the strategic direction aligns with the enterprise roadmap, creating blueprints that construction teams use to build a given structure. Decision making is shared between IT leaders and architects.

---

[13] "Data Mesh Principles and Logical Architecture." *Martinfowler.com*, 3 Dec. 2020, www.martinfowler.com/articles/data-mesh-principles.html.

Team	Centralized Responsibility	Federated Responsibility
Data Domain Specialists	Data domain-specific responsibility does not formally exist.	Data domain-specific stewards manage the critical data elements of a data domain. These Data Stewards are responsible for all data management and quality within the unit as well as the full lifecycle of the data.
Data Platform Core Team	The data platform custodian team is responsible for managing the infrastructure and creating and maintaining data pipelines for producers and consumers. Data models are created and maintained by the data platform data modeler on behalf of the producers and consumers to ensure alignment with platform standards and requirements.	The data platform custodian team is responsible for infrastructure and is equipped to provide technical guidance to producer and consumer custodian teams when needed. The data platform data modeler assembles data models to ensure alignment with platform standards and requirements, while its design and creation are shared responsibilities.
Consumer Team	The IT and their business teams consuming data from the data platform provide requirements to the data platform team to build the model and pipeline.	The IT and their business teams consume data from the data platform to build the model and pipeline on the data platform.
Producer Team	The IT and their business partners publishing data to the data platform provide requirements to the data platform team to build the model and pipeline.	The IT and their business partners publishing data to the data platform collaborate to build the model and pipeline on the data platform.
Onboarding Team	There is no strong need to establish this team in a centralized model.	The main responsibilities of the Onboarding team are: <ul><li>Provide guidance and advice</li><li>Ensure all required metadata is made available</li><li>Enforce platform-level standards and policies</li></ul>

Table 1: Summary of the differences and similarities between federated and centralized responsibility

Metadata Driven Development

Metadata is documentation about data. Metadata Management within the DAMA International Body of Knowledge (DMBOK) is defined as "the planning, implementation, and control activities to enable access to high quality, integrated metadata."[14] The tools and processes to support metadata management practice need to support the following different categories of metadata:

Business metadata

- Glossary
- Data quality rules
- Regulatory constraints
- Data policies

Technical metadata

- Physical data models
- Source to target mappings and transformations
- Data producing systems inventory
- Data consuming systems inventory

Data ownership

- Data steward roles
- Data owner
- Data custodian roles

Metadata helps to answer questions such as:

- What data is available?
- Which systems have the data required?

---

[14] "DMBOK - Data Management Body of Knowledge." *DAMA*, 3 Apr. 2024, www.dama.org/cpages/body-of-knowledge.

- How does the data flow through the enterprise?
- How do I get access to the data?
- Who can help me answer questions about the data I need?

In the context of a data platform, the ingestion and consumption of data need to be driven by metadata. It is the critical component that allows for the self-serve of data. Metadata-driven development means documentation is created and used as part of the lifecycle rather than after the fact. Figure 15 depicts what metadata-driven development looks like.

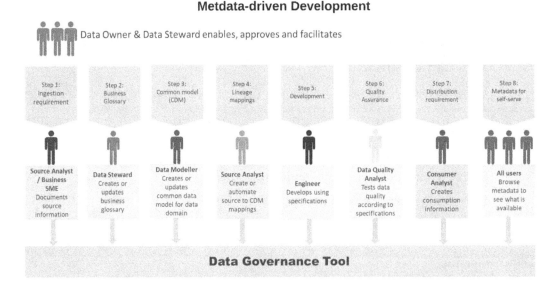

Figure 14: Metadata-driven development

Data Domain Driven Architecture

A data domain is a category of data with related data elements describing a business capability. For example, the customer data domain describes the customer holistically by capturing their name, address, phone number, email address, etc., so the enterprise has a

360° view of the customer. Data domains differ by industry. Here are some examples of the different data domains that exist in the wealth management industry:

- **Customer data domain:** This includes data related to customers, such as contact information, demographics, preferences, and purchase history.

- **Trade data domain:** Describes the trade-economic details that make up the contract between two or more parties.

- **Instrument data domain:** Describes the listed securities and their characteristics.

- **Employee data domain:** This includes data related to employees, such as job titles, roles, performance, and compensation.

- **Market data domain:** Describes the financial or economic statistical or quantitative measure that directly or indirectly influences the financial asset and is generated by an external party.

- **Reference data domain:** This includes data related to enumeration or codes and classifications used across different domains.

Data domain driven architecture requires a list of data domains to be identified and defined as a prerequisite for the data platform because these domains drive the design, development, data model, and ingestion of the data. For example, if a customer data domain is prioritized and then authorized data sources with customer data are identified, data is profiled by domain-specific analysts and requirements are created by data domain specialists to prepare the design. The development of data pipelines, data models, APIs, data storage, and so on is organized by data domain, which, in this example, is the customer. Most enterprises have made great progress in identifying and defining their data domains (even though they may be called by different names), so it should not be a long exercise to gather this information.

Data Models

The data platform comprises three layers of data models: raw, standardized, and consumer-specific. It is essential to document the types of models to be used, along with the chosen approach, and ensure this information is easily accessible. Data models serve as fundamental building blocks of the platform, and errors in their design can lead to costly refactoring later. Therefore, investing time upfront to establish clear guidelines for creating and maintaining these models is highly advisable. We will explore this topic in greater detail in a later chapter.

Patterns and Standards

When data producers publish data to the data platform and consumers retrieve it, they must adhere to established standards and patterns. This ensures the solution remains manageable and scalable, allowing for future growth and adaptability across diverse data needs.

In the decentralized approach, data producers are responsible for publishing their data to the data platform. They can choose from three different patterns for data publication:

1. **Publish to raw layer only using schema-on-read**: In this pattern, data producers publish raw data without enforcing a predefined schema. The schema is applied only when reading or processing the data, allowing maximum flexibility in handling varied and unstructured data.

2. **Publish to raw layer, then transform to CDM format in standardized layer**: Here, data is initially published to the raw layer. Subsequently, it is transformed into a standardized Common Data Model (CDM) format and moved to the

standardized layer. This pattern provides flexibility while ensuring data consistency, data quality, and compatibility for downstream consumption.

3. **Publish directly to standardized layer using schema-on-write**: This approach involves enforcing a predefined schema at the time of data ingestion, ensuring that data conforms to the required structure as it is published to the standardized layer. This pattern supports data quality and consistency from the start, making it ideal for well-defined and structured datasets.

Consumers are responsible for developing data pipelines to extract and use data from the data platform. They have the following options for data consumption:

- **Consume from raw layer**: In this method, consumers access data in its original, unprocessed form. This approach is suitable for tactical use cases where consumers need to transform or analyze raw data themselves.

- **Consume from standardized layer**: Consumers can access data that has been transformed and standardized to a consistent CDM. This option provides data that is standardized, structured, and ready for analysis or integration, reducing the complexity of data handling.

- **Consume from consumer-specific layer**: This layer offers aggregated or customized data to meet the specific needs of a consumer or application. It provides data in a format tailored for optimal performance and ease of use for specific use cases, such as business intelligence reporting or specialized analytics.

In the later chapters, we will explore the patterns and standards in more detail.

Technology Stack Selection

The architecture team should provide the list of tools the enterprise will use to govern and fit the data platform use cases. Changing technology choices halfway through development is costly, so give careful consideration to avoid refactoring. Cloud solutions are popular because they offer scalable and flexible infrastructure and solutions. Here are some instances of non-functional use cases to address for the data platform:

- Real-time and Batch integration
- ACID capabilities
- Schema-on-read and schema-on-write
- Data loss mitigation
- Data encryption and masking capabilities
- Data portability when there is an enterprise change in the governed tech stack
- Data distribution performance to meet SLAs

Here is a list of some of the popular **Data Storage and Processing** tools:

- **Amazon S3**: An object storage service for structured and unstructured data.

- **Amazon Redshift**: Sits on top of Amazon Web Services (AWS) and easily integrates with other data tools in the space.

- **Snowflake**: The original cloud data warehouse.

- **Google BigQuery**: Fully managed, AI-ready data analytics platform designed to be multi-engine, multi-format, and multi-cloud.

- **Microsoft Azure**: Azure is a cloud computing platform and an online portal that allows you to access and manage cloud services and resources provided by Microsoft.

- **Databricks**: The Databricks Lakehouse Platform is a unified, end-to-end platform that caters to data management, business analytics, and ML applications.

Ingestion solutions include:

- **Apache Kafka**: High-performance, scalable system for real-time data streaming and processing.

- **Amazon Kinesis**: A platform within Amazon Web Services (AWS) designed to collect, process, and analyze real-time, streaming data.

- **Apache NiFi**: Focuses on automated data flow between systems, supporting both streaming and batch processing with a user-friendly interface.

- **Apache Spark**: Apache Spark is used for big data workloads. It can handle both batches as well as real-time analytics and data processing workloads. Often used in conjunction with Databricks.

- **Google Cloud Dataflow**: A fully managed, serverless service for stream and batch data processing within the Google Cloud Platform.

Data Observability tools include:

- **Datadog**: Integrates real-time metrics and performance data across your full tech stack.

- **Grafana**: Enables teams to monitor their applications' performance effectively. Its flexibility in dashboard creation helps teams visualize complex data effortlessly.

- **Splunk**: Combines log management, performance monitoring, and security insights into a single platform.

- **AWS Suite**: A robust collection of monitoring tools designed to ensure comprehensive oversight of cloud operations.

These are popular **Data Catalog tools** for data governance:

- **Collibra**: Its data catalog capabilities support an extensive set of automated features for data discovery and classification using a proprietary ML algorithm; data curation, also powered by ML; and data lineage.

- **Informatica Enterprise Data Catalog**: It can automatically scan, ingest, and classify data from systems across an organization, as well as multi-cloud platforms, BI tools, ETL workflows, and third-party metadata catalogs.

- **Microsoft Purview**: A data governance, compliance, and risk management cloud service tool introduced in April 2022.

- **Alation**: Uses AI, ML, automation, and NLP techniques to simplify data discovery and automatically generate business glossaries. Alation can analyze data usage patterns to streamline data stewardship, data governance, and query optimization.

When determining a methodology, it is important to remember one size does not fit all. The data strategy, vision, roles and responsibility, metadata management, data domains, data models, and ingestion and consumption patterns, policies, and technology choices must fit the enterprise business strategy and culture. Also, getting into pages and pages of documentation is not beneficial, so it's best to keep all documentation and design to a practical level, only focusing on the documentation required to enable self-serve.

## CHAPTER FOUR

Data Model Evolution and The Common Data Model

Data models are an important part of the data platform because they are the blueprint for understanding the data. At the end of the day, data platforms are about making corporate data available for various business use cases, hence, how the data is structured and defined is important. Data modeling is the process of analyzing requirements and designing structures that can collect and store all the different data types as well as their relationships. Data modelers use text, symbols, and diagrams to visually represent the enterprise data. In a nutshell, data modeling is a process that clarifies and captures business requirements for technology and business teams, resulting in a unified view of the data.

With the introduction of the data lake in 2010 to address big data concerns, data models became perceived as a time-consuming task that frequently slowed project delivery by becoming a bottleneck. However, this perception has gradually shifted as data governance, security, and data quality have emerged as key pillars of effective data management. Today, information on data models can be somewhat confusing due to differing perspectives on their importance and best practices. Therefore, it is valuable to explore the evolution of data models and the concept of a common data model to determine the most appropriate types of data models for each layer of the data platform.

Data Modeling Concepts

Data models are core parts of data architecture and bring together all segments of an enterprise (technology, business, data office) to collaboratively design data platforms and other applications. There are three types of data models, each with a different purpose as you work through the data modeling process.

1. Conceptual data model
2. Logical data model
3. Physical data model

The objective of this section is not to teach data modeling but to provide a fast reminder of traditional data models and how to use them in an enterprise. These models were originally developed for relational databases, but many concepts remain relevant today. Figure 16 provides a good overview of the three types of data models and how they help enterprises structure their data. The table below summarizes the features of the three models.

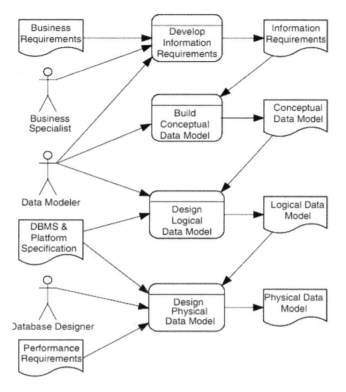

Figure 15: Conceptual, logical, and physical data model tasks and deliverables overview from Data Modeling Essentials book[15]

Table 2 below summarizes the three types of data models and their features.

	Conceptual Data Model	Logical Data Model	Physical Data Model
What is it?	Data domain-specific model captures the high-level business concepts and their relationships in a diagram format with supporting definitions.	Logical data models add more details to the conceptual model by fully defining relationships and adding data attributes to entities.	The physical data model incorporates changes required to implement the model in a technical schema focusing on performance, physical storage, and access controls.

[15] Simsion, Graeme C, and Graham C Witt. "Database Design Stages and Deliverables" *Data Modeling Essentials*, 3rd ed., Morgan Kaufmann Publishers, San Francisco, CA, 2005, p. 16.

	Conceptual Data Model	Logical Data Model	Physical Data Model
Why use it?	Provides a broad overview of a data domain and its boundaries.	Presents a clear picture of the data's structure and relationships, creating a unified view of the data. A logical data model serves as a blueprint for the physical data model.	Provides a technology-specific blueprint for scalable storage and performance that is cost-effective
Level of Detail	High-level diagram and definition. Entities and relationships for a data domain.	Adds more details to the conceptual data model. Detailed diagram with all business data elements and their definitions. Entities, attributes, keys, data types, reference data, and relationships.	Technology schema-specific details such as triggers, indexes, storage, and performance considerations are captured.
Technology dependence	Technology independent	Technology independent	Technology dependent
Elements Included			
Entity Names	✓	✓	
Entity Relationships	✓	✓	
Attributes		✓	
Primary Keys		✓	✓
Foreign Keys		✓	✓
Data Types		✓	✓
Reference Data / Enumerations		✓	✓
Table Names			✓
Column Names			✓

Table 2: Three types of data models and their features

Conceptual Data Model

The Conceptual Data Model (CDM) is a data domain-specific, technology-independent model that captures the high-level business concepts in a diagram format with supporting definitions. "They are most frequently used during the beginning of a new project, when high-level concepts and initial requirements are hashed out. Often, they are created as precursors or alternatives to the next stage: logical data models."[16] Ideally, data domains should be identified before designing the conceptual models, as these models focus on broadly defining the entities within each data domain.

The process of designing the conceptual model answers questions such as:

1. Is there a business glossary for the data domain to leverage?
2. What is the list of entities for the data domain?
3. Who are the impacted authoritative data producers?
4. How can the datasets be grouped to reflect the business?
5. Is there a relationship between the datasets?
6. Is there a hierarchy between the datasets?
7. Is the correct enterprise nomenclature followed?

Conceptual Data Model

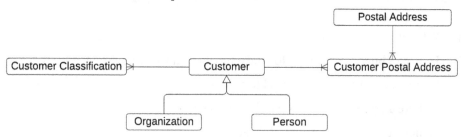

Figure 16: Simple example of a conceptual data model for customer data domain

---

[16] "What Is a Data Model?" erwin, Inc., www.erwin.com/learn/data-model.aspx. Accessed 8 Sept. 2024.

Figure 17 presents a simple example of a conceptual model for the customer data domain. While real-world customer data domains are far more complex, this basic model with a few entities illustrates modeling concepts. The data modeler comes up with a list of entities for the domain based on business requirements. The data modeler creates the diagrams and entity definition and reviews the artifacts with business stakeholders, architects, and engineers. The conceptual model should be kept up-to-date as requirements change during the development process.

Logical Data Model

Logical Data Model (LDM) adds more details to the conceptual data model. "After your problem domain and initial concepts become clearer through conceptual data modeling, it's time to get more specific with a logical data model. Whether you're looking through the lens of a single project or your entire enterprise, these models clarify the various logical entities (types or classes of data) you'll be working with, the data attributes that define those entities, and the relationships between them."[17]

When translating the conceptual model to a logical data model, the data modeler adds attributes, data types, and reference data (or enumerations) to the diagram. This process answers questions such as:

1. What data elements are needed?
2. Is there a business glossary for the data domain to leverage?
3. Is there an industry data model to leverage?
4. Is there a relationship between the datasets?
5. Is there a hierarchy between the datasets?
6. Is the correct enterprise nomenclature followed?
7. Is historical data required for the data domain?

---

[17] "What Is a Data Model?" erwin, Inc., www.erwin.com/learn/data-model.aspx. Accessed 8 Sept. 2024.

8. Are the regulatory requirements being met by the model?

9. Are the attributes data sensitivity classified accurately?

A data dictionary with entity and attribute definitions and security classification accompanies the logical data model diagram to clearly understand the model. This model and dictionary are created by the data modeler and reviewed by architects and engineers. Once the model passes all the reviews, it is time to work on the physical model. Figure 18 shows the logical data model for the customer data domain:

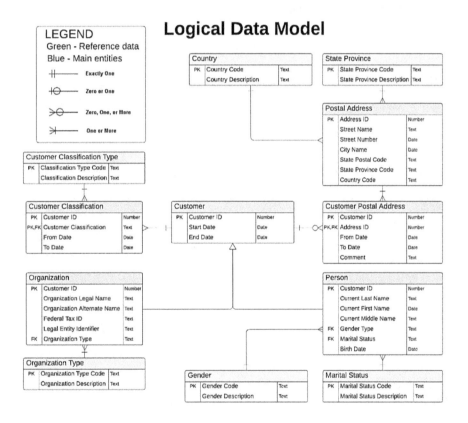

Figure 17: Simple example of a logical data model for the customer data domain. The main entities are in blue and reference data entities are in green.

Physical Data Model

The Physical Data Model (PDM) defines how the model is instantiated in a technology-specific schema. Relational databases include tables, columns, data types, indexes, triggers, and the relationships between them. "Physical data models generally are used to design three types of databases: relational for traditional operational databases, document for NoSQL and JSON databases, and dimensional for aggregation and business intelligence data stores such as data warehouses and data marts."[18] Figure 19 shows the physical data model for the customer data domain:

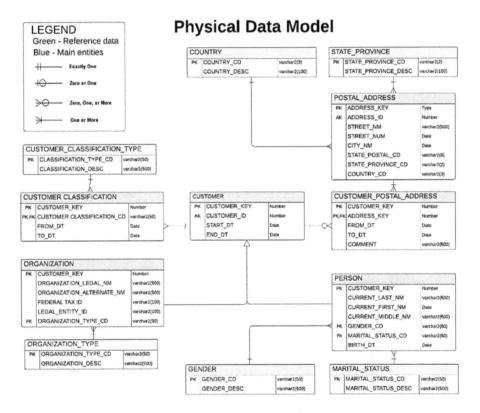

Figure 18: Physical data model for the customer data domain

---

[18] "What Is a Data Model?" erwin, Inc., www.erwin.com/learn/data-model.aspx. Accessed 8 Sept. 2024.

The data modelers or engineers translate the logical data models to technology-specific data models, considering storage and performance. This process answers questions such as:

1. What are the best tools and technology for the use case?
   a. Which solution is best for the data store?
   b. Which solution is best for the API?
   c. Which solution is best for real-time data streaming?
   d. What type of file is best for the file format integration?
2. How will data be populated? When will the data be populated?
3. What is the lineage?
4. Is there a user interface for data population?
5. How are ACID requirements satisfied?
6. Is there a need for one-time data migration?
7. What aspects of insert, update, and delete are handled by automation procedures?
   a. Error handling
   b. Audit
   c. Reconciliation
   d. Data quality check results
   e. Operational reports

In a relational database, tables and columns are defined following physical model standards, indexes are included, and triggers and stored procedures are developed if required. In the example in Figure 19, surrogate keys are added to the tables to decouple them from natural or business keys. Surrogate keys are artificially manufactured identifiers that uniquely identify a record, as opposed to natural keys, which have business meaning and may change. Once the physical model is complete, it can be deployed to allow for data insertion, updates, and deletions as required. Like all models, it is a living artifact that must be continuously updated and kept in sync with changes to the logical data model.

Normalization

Data normalization is the process of eliminating redundancy and creating a consistent view of enterprise data. It involves applying formal rules to standardize and organize data, eliminating anomalies that compromise data quality. The result is clean, well-structured data that is easier to group, interpret, and manage. Without normalization, data duplication occurs, making governance more challenging. A brief description of the five normalization rules appears below.

First Normal Form (1NF)

- No repeating entities or attributes, every attribute depends on the primary key.
- Each entity has a valid primary key.
- Removes repeating groups.
- Each data entry can have only a single value for each cell, and each record must be unique.

Second Normal Form (2NF)

- 1NF rule must be fully applied before 2NF can be applied.
- Eliminates duplicate data entry, creates separate entities, and links them using foreign key.
- Each entity has a primary key and every attribute depends on that primary key.

Third Normal Form (3NF)

- 1NF and 2NF rules must be fully applied before 3NF can be applied.

- Each attribute depends on no attributes outside the key. The famous saying is "The key, the whole key, and nothing but the key".
- This is the commonly desired normalization state.

Fourth Normal Form (4NF)

- 1NF, 2NF and 3NF rules must be fully applied before 4NF can be applied.
- Resolves multi-value facts by separating the data into different entities, minimizing null values in the data.
- This normalization is not commonly used.

Fifth Normal Form (5NF)

- 1NF, 2NF, 3NF and 4NF rules must be fully applied before 5NF can be applied.
- Data is decomposed into smaller entities using the same key.
- All join dependencies use parts of the primary key.
- This normalization is not commonly used.

Data Modeling Techniques

Data modeling techniques refer to various approaches used to design data models. These techniques dictate rules and standards the data modeler must follow when defining the data structures and their relationships. Below are some commonly used data modeling techniques.

Entity-Relationship Diagram (ERD)

The Entity-Relationship Diagram (ERD) is one of the most widely used data modeling techniques. It visually represents entities, attributes, and the relationships between them. Peter Chen developed ERDs in the 1970s. "His entity relationship model was a way to visualize a database that unified other existing models into a single understanding that removed ambiguities."[19] The model makes use of First Normal Form (1NF), Second Normal Form (2NF), or Third Normal Form (3NF) normalization rules to achieve consistency. Chen's style of diagraming is called Chen's notation. Since then, there have been other data modeling notations such as Crow's Foot, Barkers, IDEF1X, etc.[20] Models shown in Figures 17, 18, and 19 are created using the ERD technique in Lucid[21] with Crow's Foot notation.

Components: Entities, attributes, and relationships.

ERDs were initially created to design relational databases. In many data management practices today, ERDs are widely used in logical data models to document the enterprise's data architecture. The physical instantiation of the ERD can be done using technologies supporting relational data models, XML, JSON, YAML, etc.

Relational Model

The relational data model organizes data into relational databases consisting of tables and columns. It is the foundation for most modern database management systems (DBMS).

---

[19] "What Is an Entity Relationship Diagram (ERD)?" *SmartDraw*, www.smartdraw.com/entity-relationship-diagram/#:~:text=ERD%20stands%20for%20entity%20relationship,the%20attributes%20of%20these%20. Accessed 8 Sept. 2024.

[20] Dybka, Patrycja. "Erd Notations in Data Modeling." *Vertabelo Data Modeler*, Vertabelo, 2 Apr. 2016, www.vertabelo.com/blog/comparison-of-erd-notations/.

[21] "Diagramming Powered by Intelligence." *Lucidchart*, www.lucidchart.com/. Accessed 8 Sept. 2024.

"The relational model is the best at maintaining data consistency across applications and database copies (called instances). For example, when a customer deposits money at an ATM and then looks at the account balance on a mobile phone, the customer expects to see that deposit reflected immediately in an updated account balance. Relational databases excel at this kind of data consistency, ensuring that multiple instances of a database have the same data all the time."[22]

Components: Tables, columns, primary keys, foreign keys, and relationships.

The relational data model is a physical model used in relational databases such as Oracle, SQL Server, MSQL, and Postgres database. Ideal for structured data with clear relationships, such as customer databases or financial records. SQL language can query the data, making the data easily available to users.

Object-Oriented Data Model (OOM)

The object-oriented data model represents data as objects, similar to how objects are used in Object-Oriented Programming (OOP). Each object contains data and methods that define its behavior. Typically, UML notation is used to design Object-Oriented data models.

Components: Objects, classes, inheritance, and polymorphism.

Object-oriented databases, such as db4o, Versant, and Objectivity/DB, use object-oriented data models. However, these models have never become popular among data modelers and are rarely utilized.

---

[22] "Diagramming Powered by Intelligence." *Lucidchart*, www.lucidchart.com/. Accessed 8 Sept. 2024.

Dimensional Model

Ralph Kimball introduced the data warehouse and business intelligence industry to dimensional modeling in 1996 with his book, *The Data Warehouse Toolkit.*[23] Commonly used in the data mart layer of the data warehouse, the dimensional model organizes data into facts (measures) and dimensions (context for facts). The data modeler typically uses either a star or snowflake schema to denormalize the data for faster slicing and dicing in reporting and analytics. The simpler, denormalized structure of dimensional data modeling offers better query performance compared to normalized models. However, a drawback of this technique is that it is less flexible and harder to extend for new business requirements compared to a 3NF data model.

Components: Fact tables, dimension tables, star schema, and snowflake schema.

Dimensional models, which can be logical or physical data models, are ideally suited and commonly utilized in business intelligence (BI), data warehousing (DW), and distribution layers of data platforms. Since these models are used in Relational databases, SQL language can used to query the data, making the data easily available to users.

Hierarchical Model

This model organizes data into a tree-like structure, where each record has a single parent and potentially many children.

Components: Nodes (records), parent-child relationships.

---

[23] Kimball, Ralph. The Data Warehouse Toolkit: Practical Techniques for Building Dimensional Data Warehouses, 1st. ed., Wiley, New York, NY, 1996.

Useful for representing hierarchical data, such as organizational structures, file systems, and evolutionary relationships among species. It is also used in mainframe databases. This is not one of the popular data modeling techniques.

Data Vault Model

The Inmon and Kimball approaches have dominated the business intelligence (BI) and data warehousing (DW) landscape for many years. Data vault has evolved these approaches to meet today's demand for flexibility and speed. In the early 2000s, Dan Linstedt introduced Data Vault 1.0, followed by Data Vault 2.0 in 2013, which provides a method and architecture for delivering a Data Analytics Service to support an enterprise's BI, data warehousing, analytics, and data science needs.[24] This modeling style combines elements of 3NF and dimensional modeling techniques uniquely suited to the evolving needs of the modern enterprise.

Components: Hubs, satellites, links

The main driver for the data vault is agility while keeping data consistent and preserving changes. Separating the stable and the temporal parts of a data model provides a great solution for that issue by making the model updateable and extensible.[25] A data vault is a physical data model, and since it is used in relational databases, SQL can be employed to query the data, making it easily accessible to users. Today, data vault models are supported by various data storage platforms, including Snowflake, Databricks, and Azure.

---

[24] "What Is Data Vault?" *Snowflake*, 23 Jan. 2024, www.snowflake.com/data-cloud-glossary/data-vault/.

[25] Ereth, Julian. "Data Vault Modeling Increase Data Warehouse Agility." *Eckerson Group*, 14 Aug. 2016, www.eckerson.com/articles/data-vault-modeling-increase-data-warehouse-agility.

Flat Data Model

The simplest denormalized form of data model, where data is organized in a single, flat table.

Components: Single table with rows and columns.

Typically used as physical data models in SQL and NoSQL databases for simple datasets or temporary storage.

Key-Value Data Model

This model represents data as key-value pairs, where each key is unique and maps to a value.

Components: Keys, values.

Typically used as physical data models in SQL and NoSQL databases for caching, session storage, and managing configuration settings.

Network Model

Network models emerged in the 1960s as an effective way to organize and represent complex data relationships. Similar to the hierarchical model but more flexible, the network model allows each record to have multiple parent and child records. The network data model uses nodes and links to provide a dynamic and flexible framework for representing interconnected information.

Components: Nodes or vertices (records), links or edges (relationships).

Network models can be logical or physical data models since they are similar to the relational model but allow more than one table to be linked. Suitable for complex relationships, such as many-to-many relationships in a telecommunications network. These models are not as widely used as the relational data models.

Graph Data Model

This model represents data as nodes (entities) and edges (relationships), often used for structuring data with complex relationships. Graph solutions focus on highly connected data required for multi-level relationship analysis.

Components: Nodes, relationships, properties, labels.

This physical data model is suitable for data with complex, interconnected relationships, such as social networks, social graphs, semantic webs, metadata, or recommendation engines that require flexibility in attribution. Cypher query language has emerged as the popular way to query Graph databases. Some vendors in this space are Neo4j, ArangoDB, Dgraph, and JanusGraph.

Challenges in Data Modeling Practice

The state of data modeling in many enterprises today is less than optimal. With the rise of Big Data, some have questioned whether data modeling is still relevant. Several factors have fueled this perception. Let's examine some of the primary reasons contributing to this view.

Outdated Approaches to Data Modeling

Adhering to the Waterfall methodology for completing the data modeling process, as outlined in Figure 16, is not practical in Agile project delivery environments, especially with new technologies where data models must be developed within sprints. Time-to-market is critical in any enterprise and when data modeling artifacts take too long to develop, the project teams find alternative ways to meet the due dates. This frequently results in analysts or engineers creating models without governance or alignment to enterprise architecture patterns, leading to inconsistent and unsustainable solutions.

Centralizing data modeling practice is no longer feasible in a world where data is rapidly expanding in both volume and significance, and business teams demand accurate, secure data to make timely decisions and gain a competitive advantage. In large enterprises, centralizing data modeling often leads to a disconnect between data modelers and project teams, which inevitably results in several challenges:

- Centralized teams often lack the subject matter expertise and access to business experts to design an accurate data model that reflects business use cases.

- Project teams often perceive centralized data modeling as a bottleneck to project delivery. The centralized structure requires teams to wait for a data modeler to be assigned, followed by additional time for the modeler to become familiar with the project before delivering a high-quality data model. If the project teams are dissatisfied with the model for any reason, they may make unauthorized modifications, leading to discrepancies between the implemented model and the version maintained by the centralized data modeling team. This misalignment undermines the value and benefits of data modeling for the enterprise.

- When data modelers are not closely associated with project teams, monitoring and maintaining good governance practices around data model evolution is difficult.

Lack of Consensus on Data Modeling Best Practice

The rapid evolution of data technologies—from traditional relational databases to NoSQL, cloud platforms, and Big Data—requires the swift adoption of diverse data modeling approaches to keep up. However, data architecture teams, typically including data modelers, are often slow to adapt to changing technologies and delivery patterns. Additionally, data modeling can be highly subjective, as there are often multiple ways to model the same dataset. As a result, teams often find themselves grappling with questions like these, unable to reach a clear consensus:

- How many data models should be maintained? Typically, enterprises must support a range of technologies, including APIs, relational databases, NoSQL data stores, Kafka, and lakehouses. This prompts the question of whether a separate conceptual, logical, and physical data model is required for each technology. As data environments evolve, techniques once deemed essential may become outdated, sparking ongoing debates about the most effective approach moving forward.

- What are the standards around translating a logical model to a physical for Cloud solutions?

- How can I best govern all the data models implemented in the enterprise?

- How can I keep metadata up-to-date as the data models evolve over time?

- How can I model reference data or enumerations for NoSQL data stores and APIs?

Outnumbered by Engineers

In an era of Cloud platforms and NoSQL, there is an endless list of tools promising fast deployment and good performance with low-maintenance data stores. "Unlike older technologies, modern cloud databases also offer powerful ways to represent complex and hierarchical data structures, such as BigQuery's nested and repeated fields. When used sensibly, these features open up new opportunities for convenient, denormalized data models. But in the wrong hands, they can also give rise to confusing and poorly structured schemas that would be better served by more conventional approaches."[26] The challenge is compounded by the fact that there are typically far more engineers than data architects or data modelers. Often, engineers without a solid understanding of core data modeling principles persuade enterprises to minimize data modeling efforts to speed up delivery. This diminishes the importance of data practitioners, leading to a situation where "data infrastructure is typically a categorical mess. ELT (Extract, Load, Transform) systems pipe in data assets from a variety of tools and applications with no context."[27] The situation is even worse in enterprises that lack formal data architecture or data modeling teams, as there are no overarching standards to ensure consistency in naming data structures, business rules, or data usage.

Data Modeling is Not Easy

Accurately designing a data model from the start using an Agile methodology is not an easy task. Most Cloud solutions and data platform vendors are not against data modeling; these vendors provide the platform and infrastructure to implement a data model. However, they leave the data modeling to their clients, who often struggle to standup a data model that

---

[26] Cooper, Aidan. "Modern Data Engineering and the Lost Art of Data Modeling." *Aidan Cooper*, Aidan Cooper, 26 Apr. 2024, www.aidancooper.co.uk/the-lost-art-of-data-modeling.

[27] Sanderson, Chad. "The Death of Data Modeling - Pt. 1." *Data Products*, Data Products, 6 June 2022, dataproducts.substack.com/p/the-death-of-data-modeling-pt-1.

satisfies their business lines and use cases. "A well-executed data model presents a seamless picture of complex properties and relationships, but designing one is much harder than it looks. It's no secret that data platform companies deploy engineers to their customers (at great expense), knowing that companies will butcher defining their own data models if left to their own devices."[28]

Data Modeling Tools

Finding suitable data modeling tools for technologies like JSON and Kafka can be challenging, but there are effective tools available for logical, conceptual, and relational physical modeling:

- **Lucidchart**: Provides limited modeling features.

- **Erwin Data Modeler**: A data modeling tool for creating conceptual, logical, and physical data models.

- **ER/Studio**: Supports logical, physical, and dimensional data modeling.

- **dbt Labs**: A data transformation tool that enables data analysts to transform, model, test, and document data.

- **PowerDesigner**: A data modeling tool for creating conceptual, logical, and physical data models.

---

[28] Cooper, Aidan. "Modern Data Engineering and the Lost Art of Data Modeling." Aidan Cooper, Aidan Cooper, 26 Apr. 2024, www.aidancooper.co.uk/the-lost-art-of-data-modeling.

Common Data Model

Enterprises who understand the importance of data governance also understand the value of data models. The data modeling practice is evolving, somewhat slowly, to adapt to the changing technology and data landscape. Part of that evolution is the concept of the Common Data Model (CDM). The CDM is a standardized, generic data model designed to integrate data from all authorized data producers while being detailed enough to capture essential data elements without data loss. CDM is used in a centralized data platform to store and standardize the data in a standardized layer, ensuring consistency, accuracy, and quality. This enhances operational efficiency by reducing redundant efforts and empowers teams with good quality data for better business decisions and analytics.

CDM is not a new concept. Here are some enterprises that have successfully established CDM as a product that can be used within the enterprise as well as externally across multiple enterprises:

- Microsoft has its own version of CDM, which "provides well-defined, modular, and extensible business entities such as Account, Business Unit, Case, Contact, Lead, Opportunity, and Product, as well as interactions with vendors, workers, and customers, such as activities and service level agreements. Anyone can build on and extend CDM definitions to capture additional business-specific ideas."[29] Microsoft CDM is an open-source data model that can be used in Microsoft products such as PowerApps, Power BI, Dynamics 365, and Azure.

---

[29] "Microsoft/CDM." *GitHub*, Microsoft, www.github.com/microsoft/CDM. Accessed 9 Sept. 2024.

- U.S. National Institutes of Health has created a CDM for claims and electronic health records, which can accommodate data from different sources around the world.[30]

- The Aerospace and Defence Industries Association of Europe (ASD) partnered with the Aerospace Industries Association (AIA) to build a CDM called S-Series. "The S-Series bring together previously disconnected pieces of data into an internationally recognized order, based on Unified Modeling Language (UML). The S-Series provides both an overview of processes and analysis for creating product support data as well as a common data model for the organization and documentation of data across all product support activities."[31]

- Macquarie Bank developed a CDM standardizing data across their home and car loan domains, allowing for a consistent representation of customer information, credit history, loan details, and financial data.[32]

Approach to Common Data Model

The Common Data Model (CDM) seeks to capture a comprehensive set of reusable data elements for a data domain while simplifying some of the rigid processes associated with traditional database modeling practices. When compared to the traditional data modeling process illustrated in Figure 16, the key differences are as follows:

---

[30] "Data Standardization." *OHDSI*, Observational Health Data Sciences and Informatics, www.ohdsi.org/data-standardization. Accessed 9 Sept. 2024.

[31] "Utilizing S-Series Specifications to Optimize Operational Readiness." *Aerospace Industries Association*, 18 Jan. 2024, www.aia-aerospace.org/publications/s-series-specification-to-optimize-operational-readiness/.

[32] Liu, Ping. "How a Common Data Model Can Improve Productivity and Ensure Scalability." Medium, Macquarie Engineering Blog, 21 Dec. 2023, medium.com/macquarie-engineering-blog/how-a-common-data-model-can-improve-productivity-and-ensure-scalability-f4dd039c8262.

	Traditional modeling	Common Data Model
Agile	• Conceptual, logical, and physical data models are created and maintained using the Waterfall methodology to cover the full data domain.	• CDM starts out by capturing critical data elements and extends the model as business needs arise. • There is only one data model: CDM.
Usage	• Conceptual, logical, and physical data models can be used in transactional, analytical, and distribution use cases.	• CDM is best used to standardize data in centralized distribution architectures, such as data platforms and APIs.
Conceptual model	• Conceptual model is a mandatory step in the modeling process, and it needs to be kept up-to-date.	• Conceptual model is not a mandatory step. • Conceptual model is a useful artifact when exploring a new data domain to ensure all the entities are captured.
Diagram	• Logical data models can use any data modeling technique.	• CDM mostly uses the 3NF ERD technique, and denormalization is used where it is practical.
Publication	• Data modeler maintains and publishes the data models to the relevant teams.	• CDM is a data domain-specific product that is versioned and published by the enterprise. It is backward compatible. Teams can take the version they need.
Review	• Conceptual model is the main diagram reviewed by the business. • Logical data model is reviewed by architects and engineers.	• Since conceptual diagram often lacks the details to do an accurate review, CDM is the main diagram used for reviews. • CDM is reviewed by business SMEs, data domain specialists, architects, and engineers.
Keys	• Logical data model captures business keys.	• CDM captures the physically implemented keys, such as surrogate and business keys.
Nomenclature	• Logical model naming convention can differ from physical model.	• CDM naming is the same in the logical and physical models.

	Traditional modeling	Common Data Model
Logical model to physical model Translation	• Physical model is created by interpreting the logical model. • There can be additions to the physical model and structures can be changed to meet the performance requirements.	• CDM entities, relationships, and nomenclature cannot be changed in the physical model. • Technology-specific additions should ideally be made by introducing separate entities rather than modifying the existing CDM entities.
Reference data / Enumerations	• Each Reference data is shown as a separate entity.	• Since Reference data is often stored in the Data Catalog or its own system, the CDM marks the Reference data attributes with a special Enum type.
Requirements	• The logical model is created based on business requirements and working groups.	• The data domain specialists and business SMEs provide a list of data elements with business definitions and examples. Business data flow documents and use cases are also desirable. • Authoritative data producers can propose a data model which can be leveraged at the discretion of the data modeler. • Industry data models are leveraged wherever possible.
Data Catalog	• Not considered part of the data modeling process. The data modeler documents definitions and reference data in the data modeling tool.	• Data modeling heavily relies on metadata that is easily accessible: ✓ A list of data elements with business definitions and examples is documented. ✓ Reference data is documented. ✓ Data dictionary is published along with the diagram. ✓ Data security classification is captured. ✓ Data producer team captures the source to CDM lineage documentation. ✓ Data consumer team captures the CDM to consumer lineage documentation.

Table 3: Traditional data model versus CDM

CDM adopts many traditional data modeling practices and evolves them to adapt to the latest needs of enterprises: faster delivery, performance, and governed data.

Benefits of a Common Data Model

- The CDM is a well-defined intuitive data model featuring extensible business entities organized by data domains, making them self-describing for users.

- The CDM is developed collaboratively with data domain specialists, business users, subject matter experts, and architects. This approach ensures the model is trustworthy and fit for use, reducing the need for costly refactoring.

- The CDM provides a unified single view of the enterprise's data domains, increasing operational efficiency, boosting decision-making, and optimizing outcomes. This leads to a higher level of effectiveness, agility, and efficiency, giving a competitive edge.

- The CDM serves as a shared data language that facilitates interoperability, consisting of standardized fields common across authoritative data producers. Without a CDM, data sharing becomes challenging and inefficient.

- The users of the CDM self-serve what they need by integrating the entities and data elements they need for their project. "Life becomes way easier if one can just take an existing model with all the problems above solved, the model battle-tested for years by high-scale business accounts, the model which is well maintained and regularly updated following all upcoming trends and demands, the model that tightly interconnects various business domains into one common data model."[33]

---

[33] Mykhailiuk, Andrii. "Common Data Model in Microsoft Fabric." *LinkedIn*, 12 June 2023, www.linkedin.com/pulse/common-data-model-microsoft-fabric-andrii-mykhailiuk/.

Standards for Common Data Model

The CDM is developed using a federated methodology, with collaboration between architects, business users, subject matter experts, and data domain specialists. While the data modeler assembles the model, the input is a collective effort. Therefore, it is crucial to document the standards that guide the CDM to ensure everyone is aligned and in agreement. Also, having a predefined set of standards that all teams have agreed on goes a long way in minimizing disagreements and unnecessary meetings. In this section, examples of standards are provided for guidance. Please note that these standards are not exhaustive and are intended only as examples.

CDM Best Practices

This section outlines the best practices for creating the CDM.

#	Best Practice
1	The content of the CDM for a data domain is obtained by merging applicable industry information and data model standards and input from business and data experts into a single, converged model.
2	The model is intuitive, easy to understand, and provides clarity on content. The model structures the information clearly and provides a business-friendly data dictionary for each entity and attribute. Overly complex CDMs are difficult to understand and maintain, leading to confusion among engineers and data users, making it challenging to derive value from the CDM.
3	A common nomenclature and vocabulary are used in the model. The vocabulary from the business glossary is leveraged where possible.
3	The base data model strives for 3NF where it makes sense. When a concept is independent and evolves over time independent of other entities, it must be normalized. However, at the discretion of the data modeler, the model can be denormalized for performance.
4	CDM is source agnostic, reflecting the business use cases and having the ability to filter and link data between entities.
5	The modeling work commences when business data elements from data domain specialists and SMEs are clearly understood.

#	Best Practice
6	The model must be stable, reusable, functionally extendable, and scalable. The base model must be based on a complete set of critical data elements for the data domain to achieve these goals.
7	All common attributes and cross-domain linking attributes are captured where necessary.
8	The CDM data structures are designed to support multiple inbound authoritative data sources. This design protects CDM from changes in source applications and keeps the design flexible for future enhancements.
9	Fields from data producers are never used as primary keys in the model to preserve independence and future enhancements.
10	CDM reflects the entities and attributes of the business, not the physical representation of a single application or a file.

Table 4: Best practices for creating the CDM.

CDM Naming Standards

This section outlines the best practices for naming the entities and attributes in the CDM.

#	Best Practice
1	The names from the business glossary are used as the first choice wherever possible.
2	All entities and attributes are named using camel case format, capitalizing the first character. The only exception is JSON, which can use camel case without capitalizing the first letter.
3	The names of systems are not used in attribute naming to ensure that the model is future-proof to system changes.
4	All tables and attributes are in full English with no abbreviation of words. For example, "description" will not be shortened to "desc."
5	Logical and physical data model entity and attribute naming standards are the same. Physical models like JSON, file, and SQL Server allow for a long length. Thus, the expectation is to follow CDM naming standards without abbreviations. Below are some examples: StartDate CurrentFirstName CurrentLastName

#	Best Practice
6	Class words in logical and physical models are always stated in the model. In general, the following data types and class words are sufficient for the model. However, more precise data type length can be used to enforce data quality:

Attribute Type	Class Word	Data Type
Name Fields	Name	Text
Code Fields	Code	Text
Reference or Enumeration	Code	Enum
Description Fields	Description	Text
Comment Fields	Text	Text
Flag or Indicator Fields	Indicator	Text
Date Fields	Date	Date
Date and Time Fields	DateTime	DateTime
Number Fields	Number	Text
Quantity Fields	Quantity	Text
Count Fields	Count	Text
Identifier Fields	ID	Text
Primary Keys	Key	Number
Type Fields	Type	Text
Amount Decimal Fields	Amount	Number
Rate & other Decimal Fields	Value	Number
Price Decimal Fields	Price	Number
Percent Decimal Fields	Percent	Number

#	Best Practice
7	All date fields have the format YYYY-MM-DD unless there is an exception specified in the documentation. When the correct format is not received from the source, the mappings correct the format to the standard format. The Date Time is specified in the following form "YYYY-MM-DD hh:mm:ss.mmm."

Table 5: Best practices for naming the entities and attributes in the CDM.

Reference Data (Enumeration) Standards

Reference data is a finite list of governed business values such as country and currency codes. Reference data is also known as schemes, domains, or enumerations. Reference data values are important for standardizing and improving data quality across multiple sources so they need to be governed centrally and carefully. This section outlines the best practices for Reference data used in the CDM.

#	Standard
1	To qualify as Reference data, the data set must be finite and static (never changing) and reusable by more than two entities. There must also be more than two possible values.
2	Reference data and their values are never deleted. They are marked obsolete.
3	Only unique codes are published to consumers of the data platform. Duplicate Reference data are not allowed.
4	Data producer-specific enumerations are not necessarily adopted "as is." To be qualified as centrally maintained Reference data, we need a business requirement from data domain specialists or business SMEs, and this element requires a control list of valid values.
5	Flag or Indicators are Reference data with the following possible values: True, False, Not Applicable, Unknown.
6	Default Reference data value "Unknown" is used when there is a known data quality issue in the data producer, and they cannot populate a Reference data value.
7	When there is an industry-standard list, it is leveraged. For example, country, currency, and language codes use ISO standards.

Table 6: Best practices for Reference data used in the CDM

CDM Evolution

Let's outline the best practices for handling CDM evolution in production. These apply within a major version of CDM, such as 1.0. This means the introduction of the 2.0 major version is a breaking change, and consumers need to upgrade if they want the new features.

#	Model Evolution
1	Within a major version, the CDM is backward compatible to insulate the consumers from model changes.
2	CDM general availability versions do not drop or rename attributes or entities used by consumers. Instead, they are marked obsolete in the data dictionary. This is done to maintain backward compatibility.
3	The model is enhanced by adding mandatory or non mandatory attributes, or new entities.
4	Back-filling of data is not preferred but when required, a new version of the records is created. To maintain traceability, data that has already been published is never altered.
5	Consumers wanting changes must upgrade to the latest CDM version. The CDM moves forward linearly, and changes are made only in the latest version.
6	Table 8 captures possible CDM changes and consumer impact.

Table 7: Best practices for model evolution

Change	CDM - Physical Data Model Change	Data Producer Reprocessing	Consumer Insulated?	Consumer Impact
Add optional attributes	JSON - Add tags Flat files - Add columns at end DB - Add nullable column	Take the new CDM. Populating the new attribute.	Yes	JSON - Recompile using new schema Flat files - Ignore columns at end if they are not needed.
Add mandatory attributes	JSON - Add tags Flat files - Add columns at end DB - Add nullable column	Take the new CDM. Populating the new attribute.	Yes	JSON - Recompile using new schema Flat files - Ignore columns at end if they are not needed.
Mark an attribute as deleted	No change. Attribute is marked as obsolete in dictionary.	Data population for the field is removed	No	There is data population change. Consumer sign-off required.
Attribute definition change	No change. Attribute is marked as obsolete in dictionary.	No change. This is a dictionary only change.	Yes	Read updated documentation that is published with the CDM
Mark Reference data as deleted	No change. Attribute is marked as obsolete in dictionary.	Data population for the field is removed	No	There is data population change. Consumer sign-off required.
Adding a new value to Reference data	No change to physical model because the field remains the same.	Take the new CDM. Populate the new value.	No	No schema changes but there is data population change. Consumer sign-off required.required.Consumer sign-off required.
Business Rule change	No change to physical model because the field remains the same.	Update the data population logic.	No	No schema changes but there is data population change. Consumer sign-off required.

Table 8: CDM changes and consumer impact

Example of a CDM

Building on the example of the Customer data domain discussed earlier in this chapter, the CDM version is illustrated in Figure 20. This CDM uses the 3NF with ERD technique and is not significantly different from a traditional ERD logical data model. However, subtle distinctions blur the lines between a traditional logical data model and a physical data model, aiming to minimize the translation required between the two. The goal of simplifying and federating the model is to meet delivery timelines without compromising the advantages of a well-structured data model. This CDM can be translated into various physical data models.

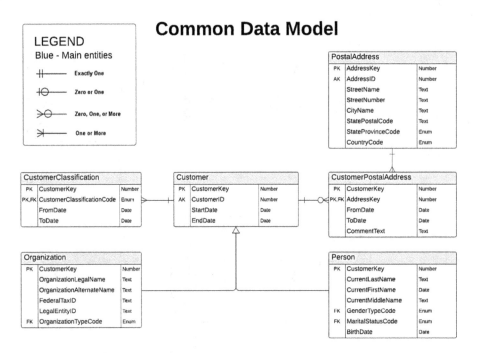

Figure 19: Simple Example of Customer data domain in CDM format

The following sections provide examples of the Customer CDM as depicted in Figure 20, translated into JSON document, Postgres relational model, Neo4j graph model, and data vault model.

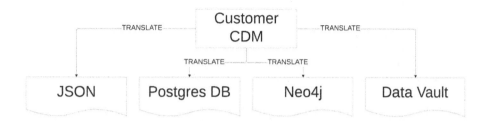

Figure 20: Customer CDM can be translated into many physical models such as JSON, Postgres, Neo4j, and data vault physical models

Customer CDM Translated to JSON Document

JSON documents have become a popular way to store and exchange data. NoSQL technologies such as Kafka, ElasticSearch, and Postgres offer JSON document storage. The example in Figure 22 is the Customer CDM in JSON format.

- The customerKey is not repeated in every entity even though they are part of the schema defined in YAML or JSON. This document uses the JSON feature to hide unpopulated fields in JSON. In this example, repeating the customerKey degrades the document's look and feel since customerKey 123456 applies to all the entities in this document, and it is sufficient to have it only at the Customer entity level.

- All the names are exactly the same as Customer CDM but in order to follow JSON standards, Camel case is used without capitalizing the first letter.

- All the relationships match the relationships shown in the Customer CDM example in Figure 20.

- The Organization entity is empty because, in the CDM, Customer has two possible subtypes: Person or Organization. Therefore, only one subtype is populated in a JSON document.

```
{
        "Customer": {
                "customerKey": 123456,
                "customerID": "HAM2344,"
                "startDate": "2023-01-19,"
                "endDate": "null,"
                "CustomerClassification": [
                        {
                                "customerClassificationCode": "Gold,"
                                "fromDate": "2023-01-19,"
                                "toDate": "2024-01-19"
                        },
                        {
                                "customerClassificationCode": "Platinum,"
                                "fromDate": "2024-01-19,"
                                "toDate": "null"
                        }
                ],
                "Organization": {},
                "Person": {
                        "currentLastName": "Hamilton,"
                        "currentFirstName": "Tom,"
                        "currentMiddleName": "Smith,"
                        "genderTypeCode": "Male,"
                        "maritalStatusCode": "NotMarried,"
                        "birthDate": "1980-01-23,"
                        "PostalAddress": [
                                {
                                        "addressID": 99282342,
                                        "streetName": "King St W,"
                                        "streetNumber": "130,"
                                        "cityName": "Toronto,"
                                        "statePostalCode": "M5X 2A2,"
                                        "stateProvinceCode": "ON,"
                                        "countryCode": "CA,"
                                        "customerPostalAddress": {
                                                "fromDate": "2023-01-19,"
                                                "toDate": "null,"
                                                "commentText": "Current residence"
                                        }
                                }
                        ]
                }
        }
}
```

Figure 21: Customer CDM translated to JSON Document

Customer CDM Translated to Postgres Relational Database

Postgres is a popular relational database. In 2023, "more than 70% of the 76,000-plus developers who took the survey said they used Postgres, which is mind-blowing when you think about it"[34] because relational databases remain a popular choice in IT despite the advances in NoSQL technology. The example in Figure 23 shows the partial DDL and Postgres tables for the Customer CDM.

- Data modeling tools such as PowerDesigner and Erwin have features that easily translate any logical data model diagram into a physical Postgres diagram and generate the associated DDL. The DDL can be shared with the engineer, DBA, or DevOps team to create the Postgres tables.

- CDM Entities are translated to tables and attributes are translated to columns without changing names or adding anything that is not part of the CDM.

- Foreign keys become RDBMS foreign key constraints.

- DevOps or DBA teams can add indexes to any column(s) to enhance search performance. Triggers and Stored procedures can be added as required.

---

[34] Woodie, Alex. "Postgres Rolls into 2024 with Massive Momentum. Can It Keep It Up?" *Datanami*, 3 Jan. 2024, www.datanami.com/2024/01/03/postgres-rolls-into-2024-with-massive-momentum-can-it-keep-it-up/.

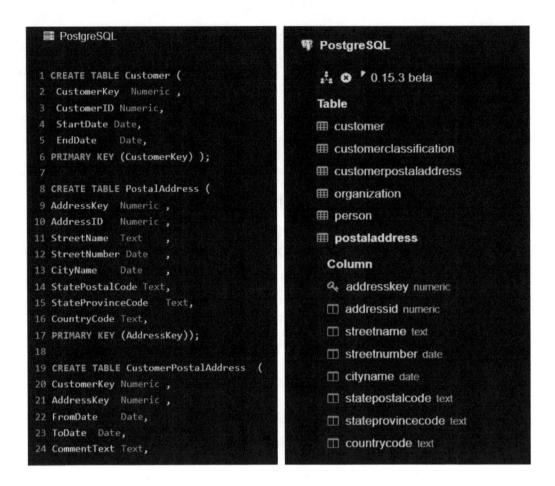

Figure 22: The image on the left is partial DDL for the Customer CDM, and the image on the right shows the six entities translated to Postgres tables

Customer CDM Translated to Data Vault Data Model

The data vault model is an option offered by vendors such as Snowflake for lakehouse or data warehouse implementations. Figure 24 shows the data vault physical data model for

Customer CDM translated to Hub, Satellite, and Links. Field-level translation is illustrated following the nomenclature described in BI-INSIDER article written by Adam Getz.[35]

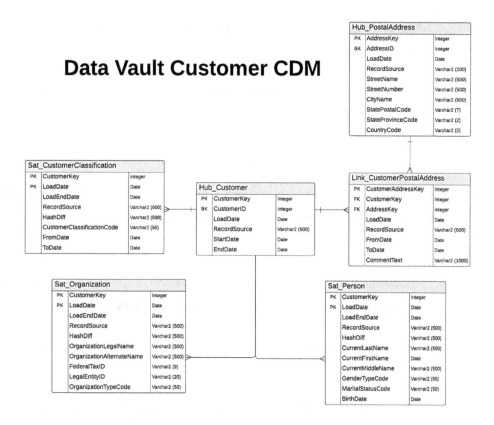

Figure 23: Customer CDM translated to data vault hub, satellites, and links

- In order to keep the data vault standards, a prefix is added to entities to mark Hub, Satellites, and Links.

- Data vault-specific attributes are added to the Hub tables PostalAddress and Customer:

[35] Getz, Adam. "Data Vault Data Model for Edw." *BI / DW Insider*, 27 Apr. 2021, www.bi-insider.com/data-warehousing/data-vault-data-model-for-edw.

1. CDM attributes AddressKey and CustomerKey are implemented as Hash Keys, which serve as the primary key of the hub table in a hash format.

2. LoadDate field is added to the model to store the date and time of insertion into the hub table.

3. RecordSource field is added to store the name of the data source where the record originated.

4. Business Key is marked based on the CDM.

- Data vault-specific attributes are added to the Satellite tables CustomerClassification, Organization, and Person:

    1. CDM Parent CustomerKey is implemented as a foreign key to the Customer hub table, and LoadDate as the second primary key field indicating the date and time the satellite record was loaded.

    2. RecordSource field is added to store the name of the data source where the record originated.

    3. LoadEndDate field is added to store the date and time that the satellite record became inactive.

    4. LoadDate field is added to the model to store the date and time of insertion into the satellite table.

    5. HashDiff field is added to the model to store the hash value of all of the descriptive values of a record.

- Data vault-specific attributes are added to the Link table CustomePostalAddress:

1. CDM attribute CustomerAddressKey is used as Hash Key. It is the primary key of the link table.

2. CDM Foreign Key attributes are CustomerKey and AddressKey referencing the hub tables Customer and PostalAddress.

3. RecordSource field is added to store the name of the data source where the record originated.

4. The LoadDate field is added to the model to store the date and time of insertion in the link table.

5. Business Key is marked based on the CDM.

Customer CDM Translated to Neo4j Graph Database

Graph databases are excellent options for Generative AI, fraud detection, identity and access management, social networking, networks, knowledge graphs, and metadata management. Figure 25 shows a physical graph data model. Graph conventions of nodes, relationships, properties, and labels are created based on Customer CDM.

- CDM entities become Node Label - Customer, Organization, Person, CustomerClassification, CustomerPostalAddress and PostalAddress.

- Data is translated to Nodes - each row in the CDM entity becomes a node in the graph.

- CDM attributes are translated to Node Properties.

- Business keys: CustomerID and AddressID are used, and CustomerKey is not used.

- CustomerClassification is an array because Customer HAM2344 has two classifications.

- Foreign keys are shown as relationships.

- Graph schemas can be highly normalized, so duplicate data in denormalized tables can be moved into separate nodes to create a cleaner model. Since Customer CDM is in 3NF, we don't have denormalized entities in this example.

- Foreign keys become relationship property existence constraints.

- DevOps team can add more constraints/indexes to business keys to enhance search performance.

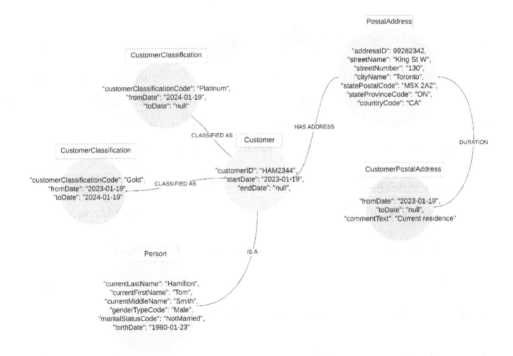

Figure 24: The physical graph data model for the Customer CDM

## CHAPTER FIVE

Data Platform Layers

The foundational layers of a data platform—raw, standardized, and consumer-specific—offer a robust and structured framework for data engineering and architecture. These layers organize and process data in distinct stages, with each serving a unique purpose to enhance data quality, performance, and governance. Collectively, they represent a data architecture pattern designed to optimize data organization and processing. Each layer is tailored to support specific types of data models and can be implemented using a variety of technology solutions, whether in public or private cloud environments or on-premise infrastructure.

This layered approach is a well-established principle in traditional data management. For instance, Inmon's Corporate Data Factory employs a staging layer, a 3NF data warehouse layer, and a data mart layer to progressively standardize and deliver data. Similarly, modern solutions like Databricks' lakehouse medallion architecture organize data into bronze, silver, and gold zones, offering a structured framework for efficient data processing and consumption.

In the decentralized data platform, data producers are responsible for publishing their data to the data platform. They can choose from three different patterns for data publication:

1. **Publish to raw layer only using schema-on-read**: Data producers publish raw data without enforcing a predefined schema in this pattern. The schema is

applied only when the data is read or processed, allowing maximum flexibility in handling varied and unstructured data.

2. **Publish to raw layer, then transform to CDM format in standardized layer**: Here, data is initially published to the raw layer. Subsequently, it is transformed into a standardized Common Data Model (CDM) format in the standardized layer. This pattern provides flexibility while ensuring data consistency, data quality, and compatibility for downstream consumption.

3. **Publish directly to standardized layer using schema-on-write**: This approach involves enforcing a predefined schema at the time of data ingestion, ensuring that data conforms to the required structure as it is published to the standardized layer. This pattern supports data quality and consistency from the start while minimizing data copies, making it ideal for well-defined and structured datasets.

Consumers are responsible for developing data pipelines to extract and use data from the data platform. They have the following options for data consumption:

1. **Consume from raw layer**: In this method, consumers access data in its original, unprocessed form. This approach is suitable for tactical use cases where consumers need to transform or analyze raw data themselves.

2. **Consume from standardized layer**: Consumers can access data that has been transformed and standardized to a consistent CDM. This option provides good quality data that is standardized, structured, and ready for analysis or integration, reducing the complexity of data handling.

3. **Consume from consumer-specific layer**: This layer offers aggregated or customized data to meet the specific needs of a consumer or application. It provides data in a format tailored for optimal performance and ease of use for specific use cases, such as business intelligence reporting or specialized analytics.

When data producers publish data to the data platform layers (raw, standardized, consumer-specific), they must adhere to established rules and patterns to ensure consistency and compatibility. These standards should be clearly documented and easily accessible to everyone within the enterprise, ensuring all stakeholders follow a unified approach when handling and ingesting data. The sections below outline some recommended standards; however, it's important to recognize that standards can vary from enterprise to enterprise. It is crucial to thoroughly assess all relevant use cases and adjust the standards to ensure they meet the unique needs of the enterprise.

Raw Layer

The raw layer, also known as the Landing area, is designed to store data from data-producing systems in its native, unprocessed format. Data is typically stored in formats such as CSV, JSON, XML, or Parquet files. Data in the raw layer can be structured, semi-structured, or unstructured, and is ingested from data producers via batch or streaming processes. Figure 26 illustrates the raw layer within the data platform.

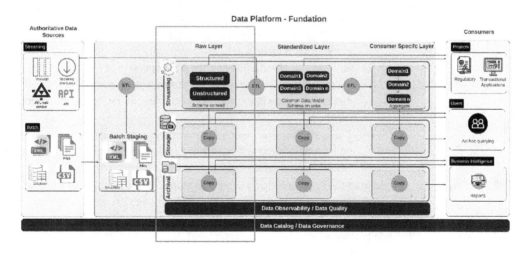

Figure 25: The raw layer highlighted in the data platform

Data Publishing Pattern and Standards

The data producer can publish to the raw layer, skipping the standardized and consumer-specific layers.

Data Publishing Pattern: Publish to Raw Layer

Figure 26: A pattern for data publishing to the raw layer

Table 9 below captures recommended standards for publishing data to the raw layer.

#	Layer	Standard
1	Raw Ingestion	The raw layer is optional and should only be utilized when a valid use case exists. Here are scenarios where it is beneficial to leverage the raw layer: <ul><li>There may be a need to store and publish technical data, like error logs, where the information does not have business relevance and does not benefit from transformations. In such cases, keeping the data in its raw format is often more efficient and practical.</li><li>The data producer cannot provide traceability, so keeping a copy of the data feed for audit is necessary.</li><li>The data producer cannot publish the data directly to the standardized layer due to the complexity of the data, making incremental standardization the best option. For example, MQ message queues from IBM Mainframe systems might be stored in this layer before being transformed or published to the standardized layer.</li><li>The data producer needs to deliver a tactical solution to the consumer to meet tight delivery dates. Publishing to the raw layer is faster than transforming the data into a standardized layer.</li></ul>
2	Raw Ingestion	Data from the data-producing system is stored in its native, unprocessed format. Schema can be automatically inferred based on feed. Denormalized flattened data structures are acceptable.
3	Raw Ingestion	Data Elements are "lightly" governed and documented as part of Metadata Management.

#	Layer	Standard
4	Raw Ingestion	The data is stored in its most raw form, often semi-structured or unstructured, with potential duplicates, errors, or inconsistencies.
5	Raw Ingestion	Data can be published to the data platform in real-time (streaming) or in batches (bulk).
6	Raw Ingestion	Error handling and auditing must be implemented to detect errors and enable ongoing support.

Table 9: Recommended standards for publishing data to the raw layer

Consumption Patterns and Standards

Consumers can directly access data from the raw layer when it is deemed acceptable under the established data standards and Steering Committee.

Data Consumption Pattern: Consume from Raw Layer

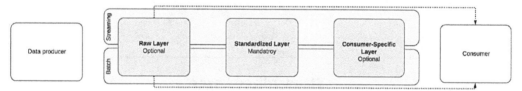

Figure 27: Pattern illustrating the consumption from the raw layer

Table 10 below captures recommended standards for consuming from the raw layer.

#	Layer	Standard
1	Raw - Consumption	Data Consumers are responsible for identifying and implementing the correct pattern for their use case. <ul><li>Consumer analysts can self-serve using metadata and data profiling. If that is insufficient, data producers and data domain specialists can be consulted for further clarification.</li><li>Communication and collaboration with the data producer team, data domain specialists, and architects need to be initiated by the consumer team. The onboarding team can assist with the coordination effort.</li><li>Data profiling must be completed to ensure data is fit for purpose.</li></ul>

#	Layer	Standard
2	Raw - Consumption	Consumption from the raw layer is generally discouraged, as it is not the preferred pattern for data use. Consumers must be aware that data in the raw layer mirrors the producer's format and has not undergone the standardization or data quality checks provided in the standardized layer. Data in the raw layer may lack consistency, accuracy, and governance, making it less suitable for reliable analysis or decision-making.
3	Raw - Consumption	Consuming systems must maintain the integrity and quality of the data provided by the data platform.
4	Raw - Consumption	Data Consumers are responsible for maintaining appropriate security standards based on data sensitivity level.
5	Raw - Consumption	Data Elements consumed must be documented as part of Metadata Management.
6	Raw - Consumption	Data can be published to the data platform in real-time (streaming) or in batches (bulk).
7	Raw - Consumption	Error handling and auditing must be implemented to detect errors and enable ongoing support.

Table 10: Recommended standards for consuming from the raw layer

Standardized Layer

The standardized layer is the foundation for data integration, where raw data undergoes standardization, validation, and conversion into a Common Data Model (CDM). CDM provides an enterprise-wide, consistent view of critical business entities, concepts, and transactions. Data is organized by data domain within the CDM, ensuring adherence to a unified schema, format, and data type. The layer emphasizes granular storage, avoiding data aggregation while actively resolving inconsistencies and duplicate entries. By establishing a standardized structure, this layer enhances data reusability across various business lines and systems within the enterprise. Figure 29 visually depicts the role of the standardized layer within the data platform.

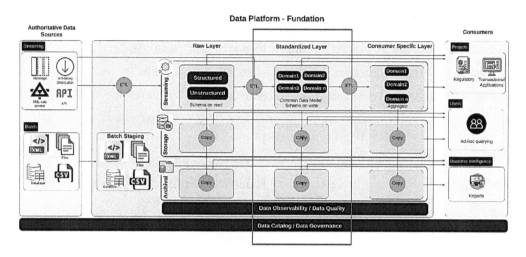

Figure 28: Illustrates the standardized layer's role within the data platform

The standardized layer is the most important layer of the data platform because it is where most of the effort goes to create meaningful data. The primary processes are as follows:

Common View of the Data

Data from multiple data producers are transformed into a common format for easy consumption. Moreover, the Common Data Model (CDM) enforces a common language, providing a common view of data from disparate sources. For example, systems A, B, and C can use different labels to refer to a client. This is confusing and requires time-consuming analysis before projects can ingest this data for their usage. To eliminate this issue, the CDM of a data platform defines a single data element with a good business definition for the client so all three systems can consistently populate the standardized data element. Now, projects wanting this data have a homogeneous common view of a client, ensuring interoperability and facilitating data analysis, reporting, and integration.

Data Standardization

While it is not the job of the data platform to match and clean the data, it does remove inconsistencies and inaccuracies in a dataset to improve its quality and reliability for analysis, integration, and decision-making. Some common tasks are:

- Standardizing data types across data producers.
- Standardizing data formats (e.g., dates, addresses, phone numbers).
- Applying enumeration or reference data to standardize constant values.
- Cleaning up data by removing empty, unused fields.

Data Domain Driven

The standardized layer is where the Common Data Model (CDM) for data domains is enforced. This means the data is stored in the most granular format, facilitating many downstream projects to consume the data and aggregate it to be fit for purpose. As the data platform becomes the single source of truth, enterprises benefit from cost savings and efficient project deliveries.

Good Quality Data

Implementing data quality checks in a centralized standardized layer is far more efficient than attempting to do so across disparate data-producing systems with varying technology stacks and source-specific fields that are often difficult to interpret. By monitoring and enhancing data quality within the data platform, enterprises can make strategic decisions and avoid costly or embarrassing data errors. Data quality checks in the standardized layer ensure that the data is accurate, consistent, and reliable. These checks typically involve validating data against established quality control measures, confirming adherence to corporate data governance policies, and resolving inconsistencies through manual intervention, cross-referencing, or business rules.

Data Publishing Patterns and Standards

Producers can choose from two possible patterns when publishing to the standardized layer. In the first pattern, the data producer publishes to the raw layer to incrementally standardize the data into the standardized layer, skipping the consumer-specific layer.

Data Publishing Pattern: Publish to Raw Layer then transform to Standardized Layer

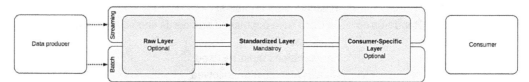

Figure 29: Data producer publishes to raw layer to incrementally standardize the data into the standardized layer

Table 11 below captures recommended standards for data publishing to the raw layer and then the standardized layer.

#	Layer	Standard
1	Raw & Standardized -Ingestion	In this pattern, the raw layer is used by data producers to incrementally standardize data before moving it to the standardized layer. This approach allows for a more controlled and stepwise transformation of data, ensuring accuracy and consistency across the various stages of the data platform.
2	Raw & Standardized -Ingestion	In the raw layer, the data is stored in its most raw form, often semi-structured or unstructured, with potential duplicates, errors, or inconsistencies. Then, it's standardized into CDM format in the standardized layer.
3	Raw & Standardized -Ingestion	The data producer should not filter out any data unless required by law. And aggregations or transformations should not be performed since granular data is required to enable the reuse of the data by multiple business areas.
4	Raw & Standardized -Ingestion	Data should be ingested from authoritative sources (original creators of that data). Intermediate pass-through sources are not allowed unless they are the authoritative data source for specific data elements.

#	Layer	Standard
5	Raw & Standardized -Ingestion	Standardized layer is a mandatory layer and cannot be bypassed.
6	Raw & Standardized -Ingestion	Since the target for the data is the standardized layer, the data is business-related and should be assigned a data domain.
7	Raw & Standardized -Ingestion	The appropriate CDM for the data domain being ingested should be used. If the data producer has multiple data domains, then the data should be separated into data domain-specific CDMs.
8	Raw & Standardized -Ingestion	Appropriate linking identifiers should be established between impacted data domains.
9	Raw & Standardized -Ingestion	All CDM data population standards should be followed. Examples: Enumerations must be used Data Types must be followed Mandatory columns must be populated
10	Raw & Standardized -Ingestion	Implement data quality checks and remediation in the Standardized layer by data producers and data domain specialists.
11	Raw & Standardized -Ingestion	Data elements must be governed and documented as part of metadata management.
12	Raw & Standardized -Ingestion	All data ingested must be comprehensive in describing the data domain holistically.
13	Raw & Standardized -Ingestion	Traceability back to the data producer should exist with metadata management. Example: Mapping documents Data flow diagrams
14	Raw & Standardized -Ingestion	Data captured in the data domain must be reconciled back to the data producer.
15	Raw & Standardized -Ingestion	The data models and data pipelines should be backward compatible to limit the impact of versioning on consumers.
16	Raw & Standardized -Ingestion	Data can be published to the data platform in real-time (streaming) or in batches (bulk).
17	Raw & Standardized -Ingestion	Error handling and auditing must be implemented to detect errors and enable ongoing support.

Table 11: Recommended standards for data publishing to the raw layer and then the standardized layer

In the second pattern, the data producer publishes directly to the standardized layer, skipping the raw and consumer-specific layers.

Data Publishing Pattern: Publish to Standardized Layer

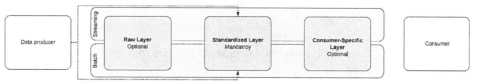

Figure 30: Data producer publishes their data straight to CDM in the standardized layer via schema-on-write

Table 12 below captures recommended standards that can apply to data producers publishing their data straight to the standardized layer, skipping the raw layer.

#	Layer	Standard
1	Standardized - ingestion	Since the target for the data is the standardized layer, the data is business-related and should be assigned a data domain.
2	Standardized - ingestion	The data producer should not filter out any data unless required by law. And aggregations or transformations should not be performed since granular data is required to enable reuse of the data by multiple business areas.
3	Standardized - ingestion	Data should be ingested from authoritative sources (original creators of that data). Intermediate pass-through sources are not allowed unless they are the authoritative data source for specific data elements.
4	Standardized - ingestion	The appropriate CDM for the data domain being ingested should be used. If the data producer has multiple data domains, then the data should be separated into data domain-specific CDMs.
5	Standardized - ingestion	Establish appropriate linking identifiers between impacted data domains.
6	Standardized - ingestion	All CDM data population standards should be followed. Examples: Enumerations must be used Data Types must be followed Mandatory columns must be populated
7	Standardized - ingestion	Data quality checks and remediation should be implemented in the standardized layer by data producers and data domain specialists.
8	Standardized - ingestion	data elements must be governed and documented as part of metadata management.
9	Standardized - ingestion	All data ingested must be comprehensive in describing the data domain holistically.
10	Standardized - ingestion	Traceability back to the data producer should exist with metadata management.

#	Layer	Standard
		Example:
		Mapping documents
		Data flow diagrams
11	Standardized - ingestion	Data captured in the data domain must be reconciled with the data producer.
12	Standardized - ingestion	The data models and data pipelines should be backward compatible to limit the versioning impact to the consumers.
13	Standardized - ingestion	Data can be published to the data platform in real-time (streaming) or in batches (bulk).
14	Standardized - ingestion	Error handling and auditing must be implemented to detect errors and enable ongoing support.

Table 12: Recommended standards that can apply to data producers publishing their data straight to the standardized layer, skipping the raw layer

Consumption Patterns and Standards

Consumers can directly access data from the standardized layer, which is one of the preferred consumption patterns.

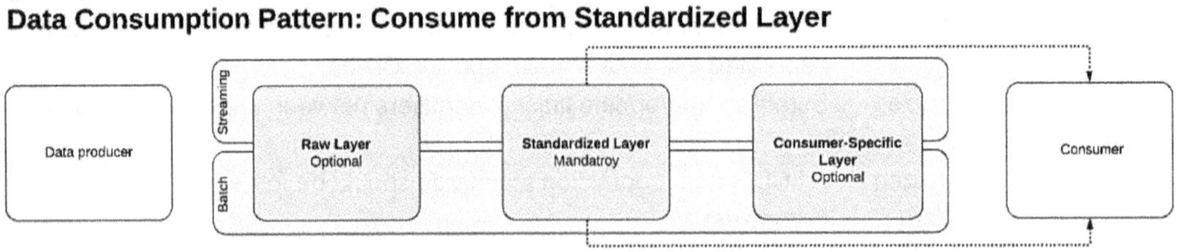

Data Consumption Pattern: Consume from Standardized Layer

Figure 31: Consumers can directly access data from the standardized layer

Table 13 below captures recommended standards for consumption from the standardized layer.

#	Layer	Standard
1	Standardized - Consumption	Data Consumers are responsible for identifying and implementing the correct pattern for their use case. • Consumer analysts can self-serve using metadata, and if that is insufficient, data producers and data domain specialists can be consulted for further clarification. • Communication and collaboration with the data producer team, data domain specialists, and architects need to be initiated by the consumer team. • Data analysis needs to be completed to make sure data meets the requirements.
2	Standardized - Consumption	Consumers must adopt defensive coding practices to protect themselves from potential changes in the producer's pipeline and schema alterations. This approach helps ensure that downstream processes remain resilient and functional, even when upstream data structures or formats are modified, thereby minimizing disruptions and safeguarding data integrity.
3	Standardized - Consumption	Consuming systems must maintain the integrity and quality of the data provided by the data platform.
4	Standardized - Consumption	Data Consumers are responsible for maintaining appropriate security standards based on data sensitivity level.
5	Standardized - Consumption	Data requirements of the consumer must be documented and gaps need to be identified. Data Elements consumed must be documented as part of Metadata Management.
6	Standardized - Consumption	Data can be published to the data platform in real-time (streaming) or in batches (bulk).
7	Standardized - Consumption	Error handling and auditing must be implemented to detect errors and enable ongoing support.

Table 13: Recommended standards for consumption from the standardized layer

Data Quality

Data quality refers to the trustworthiness of a data record concerning its intended purpose. It is influenced by several factors, including accuracy, timeliness, completeness, consistency, reliability, and relevance. Ensuring high data quality is critical in the standardized layer of the data platform, as it drives user adoption while enabling effective decision-making, analytics, and day-to-day operations within an enterprise. The raw layer stores data in its original form, which is directly sourced from the data producer. Therefore, if the data quality is high at the source, this quality will be reflected in the raw layer of the data platform and vice versa. It is essential to communicate to users of the data platform that they should not expect high-quality data in the raw layer. Conversely, the consumer-specific layer aggregates data from the standardized layer, meaning that if the quality is good in the standardized layer, it will also be reflected in the consumer-specific layer. Thus, the most effective approach to achieving high data quality is implementing rigorous quality checks and standards within the standardized layer of the data platform since the standardized data domain grouping exists in this layer.

Below are the key dimensions of data quality:

- **Accuracy**: Data must correctly describe the business it represents. For example, a customer's permanent address must be correct to enable a 360-degree view of the customer.

- **Completeness**: Data should be complete with all the critical data elements to holistically describe the data domain, meaning there is no missing information. For instance, the data is considered incomplete if a customer's primary phone number is missing.

- **Consistency**: Data should be consistent across different data collections such as files, tables, documents, etc. For example, if a customer's address differs across systems, it can lead to confusion and errors.

- **Reliability**: Data must be reliable and error-free to be deemed usable. For instance, if customer address data is not ingested from the Customer MDM system, it may not serve its intended purpose. Similarly, if errors occur from Customer MDM to the data platform during the integration process, the resulting data cannot be considered fit-for-purpose.

- **Timeliness**: Data should be readily available when required in APIs, systems, or the data platform. For instance, if the nightly loading of customer data takes too long and fails to be completed before the start of business operations, the timeliness of the data is compromised.

- **Relevance**: Data is useful for business purposes. For example, the Customer start date field should contain valid date values, and a field to capture age should contain only numbers.

Implementing a robust data quality practice in the data platform offers numerous advantages. Most importantly, high-quality data drives user trust and adoption within the enterprise, which is critical for establishing the data platform as the authoritative "golden copy" of data. When users rely on accurate, consistent, and well-governed data, they are more likely to engage with and leverage the platform for decision-making, analytics, and strategic initiatives. This trust ensures the data platform becomes a cornerstone of the enterprise's data ecosystem. Here are some additional benefits:

- **Improved decision-making**: High-quality data is essential for reporting, analytics, AI models, and everyday business operations. Poor data quality can lead to confusion, misaligned strategies, and erroneous decisions.

- **Regulatory compliance**: Accurate, well-governed data is necessary for regulatory reporting. Non-compliance with regulations can result in significant fines and reputational harm, which enterprises strive to avoid.

- **Building trust in the data platform**: Good data quality improves user experience and fosters trust in the data platform, encouraging greater participation across the organization.

Implementing data quality involves multiple steps. Here are some strategies for ensuring data quality in the data platform:

- **Authoritative data sources**: Data should be ingested into the data platform exclusively from authoritative data sources rather than intermediary systems that may introduce inaccuracies.

- **Data standardization**: Proper implementation of enumerations, Boolean values, mandatory field population, and adherence to the Common Data Model (CDM) format contributes to data standardization, enhancing overall data quality.

- **Data governance**: Establishing data sharing agreements, policies, procedures, stewardship, and data ownership fosters a data-centric culture across the enterprise, ensuring effective management of data assets.

- **Automated data quality checks**: Implementing data quality checks through tools that automatically monitor data quality and generate reports for business review leads to incremental improvements over time.

- **Data enrichment**: In the data platform, data is organized into distinct data domains; however, these domains must be linked with Master Data Management (MDM) identifiers to enhance data quality. Figure 33 illustrates an example of data enrichment using master identifiers.

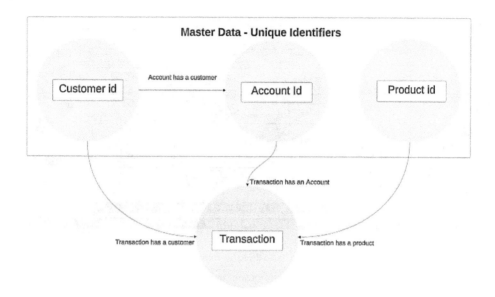

Figure 32: Illustrates an example of data enrichment using master identifiers

Consumer-Specific Layer

The consumer-specific layer, also referred to as the aggregated layer, is used to transform, combine, and aggregate multiple data domains together to meet the specific needs of end-users or consumer projects. Designed typically for reporting purposes, this layer utilizes denormalized, read-optimized data models with minimal joins, ensuring fast access to insights. It serves as the final stage for applying data transformations and quality rules, making it well-suited for Kimball's dimensional star schema, which is optimized for performance and tailored to the unique requirements of users, departments, or business processes.

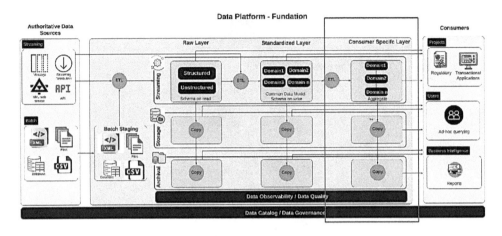

Figure 33: Illustrates the consumer-specific layer within the data platform. Consumers can use the Consumer Specific layer to merge and aggregate various data domains to suit their use cases.

The consumer-specific layer is curated by the consumer and used by the consumer. This highly curated layer often contains business-specific metrics, KPIs, and pre-aggregated datasets, providing data ready for consumption by user interfaces, dashboards, business analytics tools, and reports. By offering data in a format optimized for consumption, the consumer-specific layer ensures a smooth and efficient experience for users seeking actionable insights.

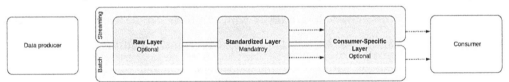

Figure 34: Consumers-Specific layer is an aggregation of multiple data domains

Table 14 captures recommended standards for using the Consumers-Specific layer.

#	Layer	Standard
1	Consumer-Specific - Consumption	Data Consumers are responsible for identifying and implementing the correct pattern for their use case. • Consumer analysts can self-serve using metadata, and if that is insufficient, data producers and data domain specialists can consult for further clarification. • Communication and collaboration with the data producer team, data domain specialists, and architects need to be initiated by the consumer team. • Data analysis needs to be completed to make sure data meets the requirements.
2	Consumer-Specific - Consumption	Consumers must adopt defensive coding practices to protect themselves from potential changes in the producer's pipeline and schema alterations. This approach helps ensure that downstream processes remain resilient and functional, even when upstream data structures or formats are modified, thereby minimizing disruptions and safeguarding data integrity.
3	Consumer-Specific - Consumption	Consumers are responsible for creating and maintaining the schema in the Consumers-Specific layer.
4	Consumer-Specific - Consumption	Consumers-Specific layer facilitates merging multiple data domain-specific CDMs to meet various consumer needs.
5	Consumer-Specific - Consumption	Transformations, aggregations, and calculations are allowed. However, these must be based on data in the standardized layer. New datasets cannot be ingested directly into the Consumers-Specific layer.
6	Consumer-Specific - Consumption	Data Consumers are responsible for maintaining appropriate security standards based on data sensitivity level.
7	Consumer-Specific - Consumption	Data requirements of the consumer must be documented and gaps identified. Data Elements, along with transformations, aggregations, and calculations, must be documented as part of Metadata Management.
8	Consumer-Specific - Consumption	Data can be published to the data platform in real time (event) or in batches (bulk).
9	Consumer-Specific - Consumption	Error handling and auditing must be implemented to detect errors and enable ongoing support.

Table 14: Recommended standards for using the Consumers-Specific layer

Data Retention

A data retention policy is a set of agreed-upon standards for retaining, archiving, and deleting the data. Enterprises establish standards based on the following information:

- Data domain identification: different categories of data need to be handled differently.

- Length of time information remains compliant with industry regulations.

- Historical data driven business use cases, such as analytics, reporting, and operations.

- Security requirements, such as Personally Identifiable Information (PII).

- Efficient storage to satisfy all the use cases.

Since each enterprise and industry possesses unique architectural and technological requirements, tailor the data retention policy to best suit the organization's specific needs. For enterprises managing large volumes of data, implementing robust data retention standards offers several advantages:

- **Regulatory compliance**: Enterprises can use the standards to enforce regulations and avoid costly fines.

- **Better data security**: Data inventory with sensitivity classification helps to store the data with appropriate security and can be deleted safely.

- **Improved data retrieval**: Data older than three years is typically accessed less frequently than more recent data. Storing data based on its retrieval frequency can optimize application and reporting performance.

- **Reduced storage costs**: Cost savings due to efficient storage design.

- **Improves access to historical data**: Older data can be separated and stored to facilitate streamlined access to projects that need it.

- **Improved reputation**: A well-defined data retention policy reflects an enterprise's commitment to responsible data management, strengthening customer trust and enhancing the organization's reputation.

The data platform should follow the enterprise standard for data retention for each layer and data domain. Figure 36 shows a sample retention standard for the data platform. The diagram illustrates that the data platform storage is separated to support data retrieval and maintenance.

- **Streaming**: Streaming data, such as in Kafka messages, is typically retained for two weeks to support troubleshooting and allow teams to review historical data for resolving integration errors if needed.

- **Data store**: Streaming and batch data are copied into a data store, such as a database or document storage, and retained for three years, as most projects typically require access to data from the past three years.

- **Archival**: Data older than three years is moved to an archival layer, such as MinIO, where active records are retained for up to seven years.

- **Purging**: Data deletion must adhere to master data and regulatory rules. For instance, in Canada, regulatory requirements dictate that all transaction records associated with a closed wealth management account must be deleted if they are older than seven years. Compliance with such regulations ensures data is properly managed and retained only for the necessary duration.

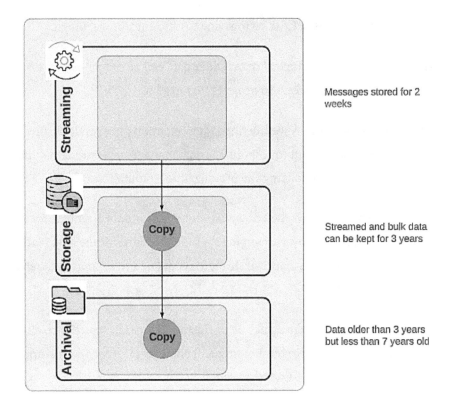

Figure 35: Data platform sample retention

## CHAPTER SIX

Consumer and Producer Onboarding

E ven in federated environments, successfully onboarding both data producers and consumers onto the data platform requires a dedicated team and a structured, well-defined process. This onboarding team plays a critical role in ensuring consistency, governance, and metadata collection while facilitating seamless integration across departments and teams. By acting as a bridge between data producers and consumers, the team enforces data standards, security protocols, and quality controls, ensuring producers can efficiently publish data and consumers can easily access and utilize it. Additionally, the onboarding process serves as an opportunity to foster collaboration, strengthen relationships across the enterprise, and drive the adoption of the data platform as a trusted, enterprise-wide resource. Figure 37 illustrates the positioning of the onboarding team within the data platform.

Data governance documents such as charter, data domain ownership, and policy documents are not within the scope of the onboarding team. Creating and getting approvals for these overarching documents are the responsibility of the data domain specialists and data office leadership team. To summarize, the main responsibilities of the onboarding team are:

- Provide guidance and advice to producers and consumers.

- Ensure all required metadata is available and collected to enhance data discoverability, governance, and usability.

- Enforce platform-level standards and policies.

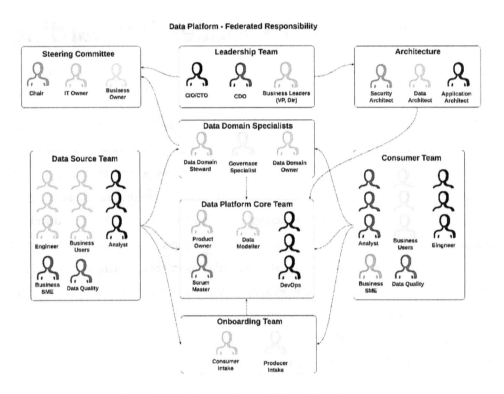

Figure 36: The data platform with the onboarding team

Consumer Onboarding

Consumers of the data platform can include both individual users and systems. Individual users often access data through APIs, download it in CSV formats, or interact with it via Business Intelligence (BI) tools for analysis and ad-hoc reporting. However, the primary focus of consumer onboarding typically lies in system integration. System integration use cases involve more complex workflows and usually require development efforts, which are best managed by the consuming team to ensure alignment with their specific requirements and infrastructure. Figure 38 provides a high-level overview of the steps involved in the consumer onboarding process.

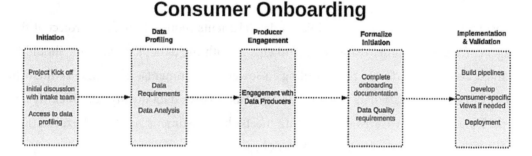

Figure 37: High level consumer onboarding steps

Here is a summary of the key steps involved in onboarding consumers to the data platform.

Initiation

The initiation step marks the first contact between new or existing consumers and the onboarding team. This is an opportunity for new consumers to ask questions, get a technical overview of the data platform, and understand the necessary processes to ensure proper project resourcing and structuring. Both new and existing consumers can use this step to explain their requirements and timelines, helping to determine the feasibility of utilizing the data platform.

This is also a good time to engage architecture if a new consumption pattern or technology stack is being considered. Data, application, and security architecture teams need to ensure architecture alignment within the data platform and across the enterprise.

For all new engagements, especially those introducing a new data domain, it's essential to engage data domain specialists and present the initiative to the steering committee. This approach ensures transparency, strategic alignment, and adequate resourcing, and provides necessary guidance, establishing a solid foundation for successful data onboarding.

Data Profiling

Consumers should have a finalized list of data elements required for their project at this stage. Once the consumer team decides to engage with the data platform, they should be granted access to perform data profiling in lower environments. This enables them to confirm if the necessary data elements are available, assess data quality, and identify any gaps. Data profiling ensures that the data meets the consumer's needs and expectations before full integration or development work begins.

Producer Engagement

If gaps are identified, the onboarding team should coordinate discussions between the consumer and the relevant data producer to address those gaps. The responsibility for working out timelines falls on both the consumer and producer teams. If the gap is relatively minor and involves only a few data elements, the producer can start their integration work while the consumer builds their pipeline. However, if the gap is substantial, the consumer may need to wait until the producer completes the necessary work.

If all required datasets are already available on the data platform, producer engagement may only be necessary to clarify specific questions that the available metadata cannot answer. Alternatively, if the consumer can locate the necessary data through data profiling and available metadata, engagement with the producer is not required.

Formalize Initiation

Once the consumer completes the data analysis, gap analysis, and planning, the data platform onboarding can be formalized. The onboarding team needs to ensure all the metadata is collected, including project details and architecture artifacts. Data quality rules for the data elements should be documented so they can be implemented once the integration is completed.

Consumer engagement with data domain specialists can happen at any stage of the onboarding process. However, at the Formalization stage, it is necessary to review the details with the data domain specialists to review any new data element and their metadata capture.

The data platform team needs to be engaged in preparing the infrastructure based on volumetrics and scalability requirements. And, if the consumer team needs technical guidance, the data platform team should be equipped to provide it in the form of training, templates, libraries, etc.

Implementation and Validation

At this stage, the consumer team can begin development work, which typically includes the creation of data pipelines, performing quality assurance, conducting user acceptance testing, and implementing data quality rules.

For consumers who are new to the data platform, challenges may arise due to unfamiliarity with the platform's technology and standards. To encourage adoption, it is essential to provide the necessary support to help them overcome these challenges. By offering guidance and ensuring clear communication, new consumers can successfully navigate and integrate the platform more effectively.

Consumer Metadata Collection

Throughout the onboarding process, the onboarding team gathers critical information about the project and its data requirements. Below is a recommended list of information that should be collected. This collection process can be automated using a marketplace technology solution or handled manually via tools like Excel or Confluence pages. Ensuring that the process is lightweight is essential to avoid making the documentation process too burdensome, thereby encouraging adoption and efficiency.

Project Level Details

Project-level details are required to give context to the data consumption from the data platform.

Metadata	Description
Project Title	The formal name of the Project Name.
Project Objective	A project description is a brief and clear summary of a project, outlining its key aspects to understand its purpose, scope, and objectives.
Project Id	The official enterprise identifier for the project.
Timeline	Key milestones or deadlines to track the project's progress. Deployment dates to various environments such as Development, User Acceptance Testing (UAT), and Production. These dates should be established in collaboration with the impacted Consumer project and the data platform team.
Consumer Application	Name of the application and ID as it is registered in the official application inventory system.
Business Processes Impacted	List of business processes or business capabilities impacted by the project.
Budget/Resources	Any financial or material resources allocated for the project (if applicable).
Architecture Diagram	An architecture diagram or Data flow diagram to understand the broader impact to the enterprise.
Tier 1 Reports	List of Tier 1 reports impacted by the project.
Countries	Listing the countries that will use the data is crucial for compliance with local and international data regulations.

Table 15: Project-level details

Consumer Contact Information

Consumer contact information is crucial in ensuring effective communication during and after the onboarding process. Here is the suggested list of information that is useful to collect.

Metadata	Description
Stakeholder Team	Line of Business, Department and group name as displayed in the enterprise organization hierarchy.
Stakeholder Owner	Names of the Director and VP of the Stakeholder Team.
Business SME	Subject Matter Experts or Business Analysts assigned to the project.
Stakeholder Contact Group Email	A distribution email list for business-related communications to keep stakeholders informed about changes and provides a single point of contact for any business-related questions or feedback.
IT Partner	Names of the Director and VP of the IT Partner. The data platform integration consumption pipeline is developed and maintained by this IT Partner.
IT Analysts	Names of the IT Analysts responsible for translating the business requirements to system-level requirements for report creation, API development, etc.
IT Partner Contact Group Email	A distribution email list for technology-related communications to keep stakeholders informed about change management and provides a single point of contact for any technology questions or feedback.
Architects	Names of the Solution Architect, Data Architect, and Security Architect assigned to the project.

Table 16: Consumer contact information

Data Feed Requirements

Consumers of the data platform list the data producers and the feed level information needed for their project. A feed can be a Hive table, Kafka topic, file name, etc.

Feed Level Metadata	Description
Data Producers	The list of Data Producer(s) required for the project. Name of the Data Producer should be the application name and ID, as it is registered in the official application inventory system.
Existing Data Platform Feed Name	List the datasets, such as tables, streaming topics, and documents that are already on the data platform and required for the project.
New Data Platform Feed Name	If there are gaps, list the new datasets the Data Producer needs to develop for the consumer.
Frequency	Indicates the frequency of the data consumption. Examples: End of Day Monday to Friday 10 pm Realtime Streaming 24/7

Table 17: Data feed requirements

Data Element Requirements

For each feed, the Consumer must document all the fields they plan to consume. If the list of fields changes over time, the onboarding team needs to be informed so the data catalog is up-to-date. Fields identified as CDE need to be documented so data quality rules can be implemented and security can be applied.

Field Level Metadata	Description
Data Platform Field Name	List the fields the consumer plans to consume for the existing data platform feed. For the new Feed being planned, it should be possible to list the fields and keep them updated if there are requirement changes.
Critical Data Element (CDE)	Indicate if the field is a CDE."CDEs may be described as the specific data needed for doing business (requiring high-quality data) or the specific data that is extremely sensitive (requiring good security). These particular data elements often have a stronger financial impact on the business than other data elements."[36]
Data Type	The data type for the field. Examples are String, Integer, Boolean, and Array of String.

Table 18: Data element requirements

---

[36] Foote, Keith D. "Critical Data Elements Explained." *DATAVERSITY*, DATAVERSITY, 29 Oct. 2024, www.dataversity.net/critical-data-elements-explained/.

Consumer Mapping – Raw layer to standardized layer to consumer-specific layer to consumer system

Source-to-target mappings play a pivotal role in data integration by defining the pathways and transformations a data field undergoes as it moves from the source to the target system. These mappings provide a structured framework to ensure data is accurately and consistently transferred between systems. They specify the alignment of each data element in the source to its corresponding target field, often detailing any transformations or business rules applied during the process.

By establishing clear mappings, teams can enhance data accuracy, maintain consistency, and support data quality objectives throughout the integration pipeline. Additionally, these mappings serve as the foundation for building robust data lineage, which tracks the flow of data from origin to destination. Data lineage can be captured manually by documenting processes or through automated lineage solutions that dynamically trace, and record data flows across systems, offering a more scalable and error-free approach.

A well-documented source-to-target mapping and lineage process is essential for compliance, troubleshooting, and ensuring trust in the data integration process.

Source to Target Mapping	Description
Producer System	The name of the data producer publishing to the data platform.
Raw layer - Feed Name (optional)	The name of the dataset, like Kafka topic, table, or file, in the raw layer. Raw layer is optional based on the chosen consumption pattern.
Raw layer - Field Name (optional)	The name of the data field in the raw layer. There should be no transformation from the Producer System to the raw layer.
Standardized layer - CDM information	The name of the Kafka topic, table, etc., in the standardized layer.
Standardized layer - CDM field Name	The original data field in the Common Data Model (CDM) in the standardized layer.
Consumer-Specific layer - Target Data Model (optional)	The target data model for the data in the data platform consumer-specific layer. The consumer-specific layer is optional based on the chosen consumption pattern.

Source to Target Mapping	Description
Consumer-Specific layer - Target Field Name (optional)	The target data field in the consumer-specific layer. Consumers can create their own data structures, such as tables and topics aggregate the CDM data into a format that suits their needs.
Target System	The target consumer system which is the ultimate destination for the data.
Target Feed Name	The name of the target Kafka topic, table, file, etc., in the consumer system.
Target Field Name	The target data field in the consumer system.
Transformations	Describes how the data is transformed between source and target. Examples: If there is no transformation, then it is a "Direct Move." The logic should be documented if default values are inserted into null fields.

Table 19: Source-to-target mappings

Data Quality

Data quality rules that the consumer plans to implement should be captured.

Data Quality Information	Description
Data Domain	Name of the data domain that requires the data quality rule. The rule is implemented in the consumer-specific and/or standardized layers of the data platform.
Feed Name	The name of the data structures, such as tables and topics.
Rule Name	Name of the data quality check.
Rule Logic	The fields that are involved in the data quality check, along with the logic applied. Example: Count of null values in the field customerName. Count of customers missing primary address.

Data Quality Information	Description
Data Quality Type	The data quality type can be specified from the following list: • Accuracy • Completeness • Consistency • Reliability • Timeliness • Relevance
Priority Scale	Criticality of the rule.
Expected Result	Description of the expected result once the data quality check is performed.
Failure Threshold	Description of the failure threshold. Example: Stop the load if 10% of the records fail.
Failure Action	Describe what to do in case of failure.

Table 20: Data quality

Producer Onboarding

Producers of the data platform are authoritative sources that generate business data that is deemed as the primary or most reliable source of information. Their data serves as the foundation upon which downstream consumers rely, making it essential for analysis, decision-making, and business processes across the organization.

Onboarding data producers based on consumer demand is a practical approach. When a consumer project requires data from the data platform, part of the project budget can be allocated to onboard the necessary data producers. This ensures that the data platform evolves in response to actual business needs, balancing immediate project requirements with long-term strategic goals. By aligning producers and consumers with the data platform's architecture, enterprises can optimize resource utilization and foster collaboration across teams, reinforcing the data platform as a strategic asset.

The onboarding steps for a data producer are different from those for consumer onboarding. Figure 39 illustrates the high-level steps involved in consumer onboarding.

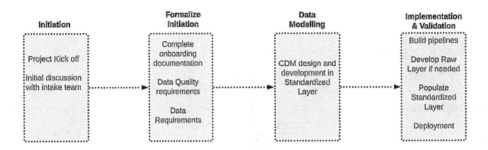

Figure 38: The high-level steps involved in consumer onboarding

Initiation

For each project, the initiation step serves as the first touchpoint between new or existing producers and the onboarding team. For new producers, it is a valuable opportunity to ask questions, gain a technical overview of the data platform, and understand the required processes, ensuring that the project is appropriately resourced and structured. Both new and existing producers can use this step to inform the onboarding team about the project needs, timeline, data domains in scope, and any infrastructure or DevOps work required.

This stage is also an ideal time to engage architecture, especially if a new ingestion pattern or technology stack is under consideration. Data, application, and security architecture teams should be involved to ensure alignment within the data platform and across the enterprise.

For all new engagements, especially those introducing a new data domain, it's essential to engage data domain specialists and present the initiative to the steering committee. This approach ensures transparency, strategic alignment, and adequate resourcing, and provides necessary guidance, establishing a solid foundation for successful data onboarding.

Formalize Initiation

Once a producer secures a committed project with an allocated budget and resources, the process of publishing data onto the data platform can officially begin. During this formalization stage, the onboarding team plays a critical role in ensuring that all necessary metadata is collected and documented. This includes detailed project information, architecture artifacts, and a clear grouping of the data to be published by its respective data domain. Furthermore, data quality rules for each data element must be defined and documented, ensuring that these rules can be implemented once the integration is complete.

Collaboration with data domain specialists is crucial during this phase. While producer engagement with these specialists can begin at any point in the onboarding process, by the time the formalization stage is reached, a comprehensive review of data domains and element specifics with the specialists is essential. This ensures that all metadata is accurately captured and aligned with enterprise standards.

Simultaneously, the data platform team must be actively involved. They must prepare the infrastructure to accommodate the expected data volumetrics and performance requirements. The data platform team should provide the necessary support if the producer team lacks certain technical expertise. This can include offering training sessions, supplying reusable templates and libraries, and sharing other relevant resources to facilitate a smooth integration process.

Data Modeling

Any data targeted for the standardized layer requires a Common Data Model (CDM) to ensure consistency and reusability across the enterprise. The scope of the modeling work can vary significantly depending on the task—standing up a new data domain or adding a large number of data elements typically involves substantial effort. Collaboration between the producer, analyst, and business subject matter experts (SMEs) is critical to creating an accurate and granular CDM serving multiple business domains. These stakeholders must provide comprehensive input to the data modeler, ensuring that all requirements are captured and reflected in the model.

The review process with business SMEs, data domain specialists, architects, and engineers is key to ensuring the model's quality and alignment with enterprise standards. However, this process can be time-intensive, particularly for complex or large-scale modeling efforts. Allocating adequate time for these reviews is essential to avoid bottlenecks. The modeling and review processes can be expedited for smaller tasks, such as adding a handful of data elements, enabling faster delivery. Once the CDM is finalized and published with a version, it can be handed off for physical model creation and implementation, ensuring the data is ready to flow into the standardized layer with the required structure and governance.

Implementation and Validation

At this stage, the producer team can begin development work, which typically includes the creation of data pipelines, performing quality assurance, conducting user acceptance testing, and implementing data quality rules.

For producers new to the data platform, challenges may arise due to unfamiliarity with the platform's technology and standards. To encourage adoption, it is essential to provide the necessary support to help them overcome these challenges. By offering guidance and ensuring clear communication, new producers can successfully navigate and integrate the platform more effectively.

Producer Metadata Collection

Throughout the onboarding process, the onboarding team collects critical information about the project and its data requirements. Below is a recommended list of information that should be collected. This collection process can be automated using a marketplace technology solution or handled manually via tools like Excel or Confluence pages. Ensuring that the process is lightweight is essential to avoid making the documentation process too burdensome, thereby encouraging adoption and efficiency.

Producer Information

Metadata	Description
Producer Application Name	Name of the application and ID as it is registered in the official application inventory system.
Timeline	Key milestones or deadlines to track the project's progress. Deployment dates to various environments such as Development, User Acceptance Testing (UAT), and Production. These dates should be established in collaboration with the impacted Consumer project and the data platform team.
IT Team (Custodian)	Line of Business, Department and group name as displayed in the enterprise organization hierarchy.
IT Analysts	Producer IT Analyst(s) assigned to the project to work with the consumer IT Analyst to ensure all the required data elements are published to the data platform.
IT Custodian Group Email	A distribution email list for business-related communications to keep stakeholders informed about change management and provides a single point of contact for any technology questions or feedback.
Business Team	Line of Business, Department and group name as displayed in the enterprise organization hierarchy.
Business SME	Name of the Subject Matter Expert(s) or Business Analyst(s) who helps to clarify business-related questions.

Table 21: Details about the data producer

Consumer Information

Details about the project or consumer driving the producer to publish data to the data platform should be gathered. However, if these consumer project details were already collected during Consumer onboarding, there's no need to duplicate this information.

Metadata	Description
Project Title	The formal name of the Project Name.
Project Objective	A project description is a brief, clear summary of a project, outlining its key aspects to give an understanding of its purpose, scope, and objectives.
Project Id	The official identifier for the project.
Consumer system	Name of the system and ID as it is registered in the official application inventory system.
Consumer Stakeholder Team	Line of Business, Department and group name as displayed in the enterprise organization hierarchy.
Business SME	Subject Matter Experts or Business Analysts assigned to the project.
IT Partner	Names of the Director and VP of the IT Partner. The data platform integration pipeline is developed and maintained by the IT Partner.
IT Analysts	Consumer IT Analyst translates the business requirements to system level requirements for report creation, API development, etc.
Business Processes Impacted	List business processes or business capabilities impacted by the project.
Tier 1 Reports	List of Tier 1 reports impacted by the project.

Table 22: Details about customer

Data Feed Requirements

The data platform's producers must be data domain-driven when publishing the data to the standardized layer. If they publish their data only to landing, data domain grouping is not required.

Feed Level Metadata	Description
Data Domain	Data domain is a grouping of data or data categories. Examples: Customer Sales Account
Raw layer - Feed Name (optional)	The names of the physical data structures in the data platform follow the naming convention standard. List of datasets such as Tables, Streaming topics, and documents. The raw layer is optional based on the chosen publishing pattern.
Standardized layer - CDM Name	The names of the physical data structures (Tables, Streaming topics, documents) in the data platform following the naming convention standard.
New/Existing Feed	Indicate whether the data feed is new or an existing one.
Feed Type	Indicate the feed type. A feed type refers to the format by which data is delivered to a platform. Examples: XML, JSON, CSV, Kafka Stream
Frequency	Indicates the frequency of the data publishing. Examples: End of Day Monday to Friday 10 pm Realtime Streaming 24/7
Countries	Listing the countries that will use the data. This is crucial for compliance with local and international data regulations.
Data Filtering	Typically, data should not be filtered since the data platform needs a full dataset. However, sometimes, there are valid reasons for filtering the data. Document all filtering. Examples: Line of business filtering Sensitive data filtering due to jurisdictional compliance
Licensing	Licensing Requirements as the result of market data. In the case of an Enterprise licence, the data can be shared freely. Otherwise, data distribution restrictions need to be enforced.
Access Requirements	System Integration and User access requirements.

Table 23: Data feed requirements

Data Element Requirements

For each feed, the Producer needs to document all the fields they plan to publish. If the list of fields changes over time, the onboarding team needs to be informed so the data catalog is up-to-date.

The data element requirements serve as an input to create the data model and to identify the CDE list, which needs to be documented to implement data quality rules and design access controls.

Field Level Metadata	Description
Field Name	The name of the data element from a business perspective.
Field Description	Business-friendly description of the field.
Field Example	For each field, add an example value for clarity of understanding.
Data Type	The data type for the field. Examples are String, Integer, Boolean, and Array of String.
Reference Data	If the field is a static list or enumeration in the producer application, provide the list of values.

Table 24: Data element requirements

Physical Data Model Dictionary

Once the data modeler completes the CDM, a version of the CDM and the data dictionary should be published.

CDM Dictionary	Description
Entity Name	List of entities grouped by Data domain. An entity represents a real-world object, concept, or system component that collects and manages data. Entities are typically key components of a data model and help define how data is structured.
Attribute Name	Each entity contains attributes, which are specific pieces of information that describe the entity.
Data Type	The type of data stored (e.g., integer, string, date).

CDM Dictionary	Description
Reference Data	If the field contains a static list of values, indicate the name of the reference data. Examples: Country Currency Customer Status
Attribute Description	A brief description explaining the meaning of each data element.
Primary key	Indicate if the field is a unique key for the entity.
Alternate or Business key	Indicate if the field contains a business unique identifier.
Relationship(s)	List the relationships between the entity and other entities.
Example	An example value for each attribute. If there are formatting expectations, document them here as well. Example: Expected format, such as "YYYY-MM-DD" for dates
Data Sensitivity	Data is often classified for each attribute. Typical categories include: 1. **Public**: Data that can be freely accessed without risk, such as public reports or marketing materials. 2. **Internal**: Data that should only be accessible within the enterprise but does not pose a significant risk if exposed, such as general business processes. 3. **Confidential**: Data restricted to specific individuals or teams within an organization, such as financial information, proprietary research, or internal communications. 4. **Restricted/Highly Sensitive**: Data that, if compromised, could cause severe harm. This includes Personally Identifiable Information (PII), financial records, intellectual property, and health records.

Table 25: Physical data model dictionary

Performance Requirements

To estimate hardware, memory, and other technical requirements, the producer must provide performance and scalability requirements.

Performance Information	Description
Response Time	The acceptable time it takes for the data platform to publish the data. This is critical for maintaining usability, especially for interactive applications.
Throughput	The number of transactions or data processing the data platform needs to handle per second, minute, or hour.
Volumetrics	Number of records per day. And the expected growth over a month and over a year.
Volume of Users	The number of users and systems expected to consume the data from the data platform.
Recovery Time Objective	The maximum acceptable time that the service can be unavailable.
Recovery Point Objective	The maximum amount of data (expressed as a period) that can be lost when a technology system or application has a failure.
Data Retention Requirement	Following the enterprise policies and practices for storing and managing data over its lifecycle indicates how long it will take to retain the data on the data platform. This strategy helps enterprises balance the need to preserve data for compliance or analytical purposes with managing storage costs and optimizing system performance.

Table 26: Performance requirements

Producer Mapping – Producer system to raw layer to standardized layer

Source-to-target mappings help ensure that data is accurately moved from the producer to the data platform by specifying how each data element in the source aligns with its equivalent in the target, often as part of a data transformation process. The data lineage can be captured manually or through an automated lineage solution.

Source to Target Mapping	Description
Producer System	The name of the data producer publishing to the data platform.
Producer System Data Structure Name	The name of the dataset (Kafka topic, table, or file) in the Producer System.
Producer System field Name	The name of the data field in the Producer System.

Source to Target Mapping	Description
Raw layer - Feed Name (optional)	The name of the dataset (Kafka topic, table, or file) in the raw layer. Raw layer is optional based on the chosen publishing pattern.
Raw layer - Field Name (optional)	The name of the data field in the raw layer. There should be no transformation from the Producer System to the Landing layer.
Standardized layer - Feed Name	The name of the dataset, Kafka topic, table, file, in the Common Data Model (CDM) in the standardized layer.
Standardized layer - Field Name	The name of the data field in the standardized layer.
Transformations between Producer to standardized layer	Describes how the data is transformed between the Producer and the standardized layer. Examples: If there is no transformation, then it is a "Direct Move." Document the logic if default values are inserted into null fields.

Table 27: Source-to-target mappings

Data Quality

Data quality rules that the producer plans to implement should be captured.

Data Quality Information	Description
Data Domain	Name of the data domain that requires the data quality rule. The rule is implemented in the consumer-specific and/or standardized layers of the data platform.
Feed Name	The name of the data structures, such as tables and documents, in the standardized layer.
Rule Name	Name of the data quality check.
Rule Logic	The fields involved in the data quality check and the logic applied. Example: Count of null values in the field customerName Count of customers missing primary address

Data Quality Information	Description
Data Quality Type	Specify the data quality type from the following list: • Accuracy • Completeness • Consistency • Reliability • Timeliness • Relevance
Priority Scale	Criticality of the rule.
Expected Result	Description of the expected result once the data quality check is performed.
Failure Threshold	Description of the failure threshold. Example: Stop the load if 10% of the records fail
Failure Action	Describe what should be done in case of failure.

Table 28: Data quality

Exception Management

The data platform serves as a strategic hub for data transmission within the enterprise, replacing the traditional point-to-point integration model. Instead, projects are encouraged to integrate the data platform into their data strategies, adhering to policies and standards set by the enterprise architecture and data governance teams. The platform's built-in capabilities and checks ensure that data producers can publish quality data efficiently for distribution to multiple downstream consumers under the principle "publish once, consume many times."

All platform users must follow established data policies and standards to maintain data reliability and integrity. However, in cases where producers or consumers cannot fully comply with these policies, exceptions may be granted. Such exceptions are carefully documented and submitted to the steering committee for awareness and approval. Typically, these exceptions come with an agreed timeline for remediation, with the long-term goal of full adherence to data policies and standards, ensuring continuous improvement in data quality and governance across the organization. When there is data debt, the onboarding team raises the concern to the Consumer and Producer leadership teams and guides them on the exception process. Below are the standards for the exception process:

- Any non-compliance with data platform policies or standards requires an approved exemption before deployment to Production, following the outlined process.

- Teams or projects seeking an exemption must document the request, including justifications, in a formal document.

- The Steering Committee reviews the exception request, providing approval as appropriate.

- Once approved, the exception request is logged with a remediation date, allowing the producer or consumer to proceed with promoting data into Production.

- The exception log undergoes a bi-annual review to track completed remediations and ensure ongoing alignment with standards.

Index